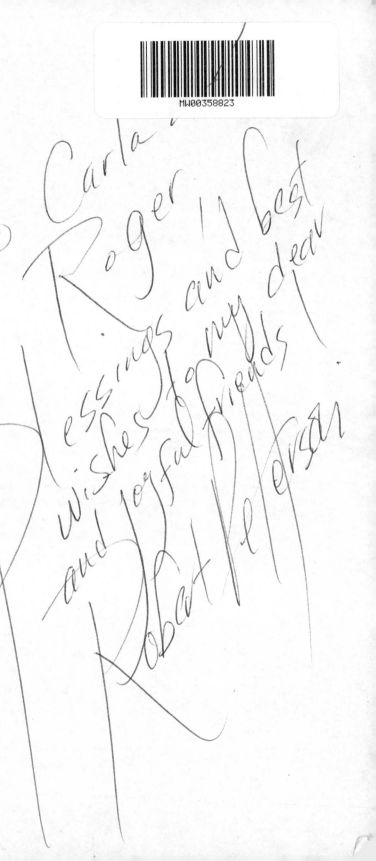

To Carla &
Roger
Blessings and best
wishes to my dear
and joyful friends

Robert Peterson

— THE THEATER OF —
ANGELS

REDEEMING AFFLICTION

ROBERT PETTERSON

PUBLISHED BY
COVENANT BOOKS

FIRST EDITION 2015

ISBN 978 0 692 58739 3

PUBLISHED BY COVENANT BOOKS
All Rights Reserved.

Comments may be directed to the author via email at:
robertpetterson@msn.com

TABLE OF CONTENTS

· TO ·

KIMBERLY CHRISTENSEN

Beloved Sister & Survivor

•••

*You continue to rise triumphant
from your ash heaps
of affliction
with grace and humor*

*Your courage amazes
and inspires me
while surely teaching
the angels
something of God's glory*

ACKNOWLEDGEMENTS

THIS BOOK HAS BEEN BIRTHED on the ash heaps of my own suffering. Like Job, I have been disappointed by comforters. Yet I have more than my share of mentors and friends who comfort me beyond what I deserve. Though I mention only a few here, I am indebted to so many more.

I am most grateful to my Lord and Savior, Jesus Christ who endured the ultimate ash heap of suffering outside Jerusalem so that I might inherit an eternal Happily Every After. I am amazed at the multitudes of God's saints who have triumphed over their ash heaps of tribulation through the amazing grace of our Creator, Redeemer, and Sustainer.

I am in awe of my dear wife and best friend, Joyce who has been my most faithful comforter through 47 years of marriage. I am a far better man because of this woman of force. I am grateful to my daughter, Rachael who challenges me to live with integrity and inspires me with her resilience.

I am further indebted to my Executive Assistant, Cindy Esposito whose cheerful competence provides invaluable support and stability to my life and work.

I am grateful to my accountability group, John, Hal, Bob, and Carl who lavish me with a rich fellowship of transparent honesty, tough love, and unfailing encouragement. I thank God for William Barnett who will not let me rest until the books in my mind are finally put down on paper, as well as Dr. Robert Palmer who has walked with me for more than 40 years.

I deeply appreciate Dave and Patti Berg for sharing their bit of Wisconsin paradise as a sanctuary for my summer writing sabbaticals. Likewise, I am grateful to Richard Breitenbücher and Claudia Lauster for extending the warm hospitality of their beautiful home in the Black Forest of Germany so that I could get away and finally finish a book that has percolated in my imagination for more than twenty years.

I find myself mesmerized by the creative artistry of Claudia Lauster whose painting graces the cover of this book. Out of our conversations about Job's ash heap sufferings came both this creation on canvas and her breathtaking sculpture of Job that forms the backdrops for the study guides at the end of each chapter of The Theater of Angels.

I am thankful to MaryAnn Lee, one of the best Bible teachers I know, for taking the time to read the raw manuscript of The Theater of Angels, and then help create this book's discussion group studies to assist the reader to draw closer to Job's God of all comfort.

Finally, I am grateful for the generosity of the elders, pastors, staff, and congregation of Covenant Church of Naples, Florida | PCA who lavish me with the time and resources to share with you what I have been privileged to teach them. For thirteen years it has been my honor and joy to be the Senior Pastor of this loving family of fully devoted followers of Jesus Christ. I am of all men most blessed!

ROBERT PETTERSON
August 2015

" All the world'
and all the m[e]
merely player[s]
their exits an[d]
and one man [in his time]
plays many p[arts]

s a stage,
n and women
s: they have
entrances;
n his time
rts. "

William Shakespeare

PROLOGUE

LIFE IS MADE UP OF many fleeting moments on the stage. Sometimes we get to be the hero. At other times we play the fool. There are scenes of high drama, snippets of comedy, and seasons of tragedy. Sometimes we may even find ourselves in the Theater of the Absurd. If given the chance, most of us would edit the script or rewrite the play.

Irish playwright, Oscar Wilde lamented, "The world is a stage, but the play is badly cast." Harold Kushner would agree with Wilde. This Jewish rabbi believed that an all powerful God writes a good script for the righteous. His optimism began to fade when his son was born with progeria, a genetic disorder that causes rapid aging in children. When his boy died as an old man at age fourteen, Kushner's faith in an all powerful and all good God collapsed under the weight of his grief.

After he buried his son, he became fixated on Job, that ancient sufferer who laid ten of his children in the grave. This obsession led to Kushner's international bestseller, *When Bad*

Things Happen to Good People. His book explores this baffling mystery: If God is powerful enough to control all things, why don't all things turn out good? Can God be both powerful and good in the face of human suffering?

He argues that an all powerful God cannot be all good. It is monstrously unfair for a righteous man like Job to endure such horrific affliction. We can cling to belief in a good God only if we abandon the dogma that he is all powerful. Kushner opts for a good God who wanted to mitigate Job's suffering, but was powerless to do so.

The rabbi postulates that some afflictions are just bad luck. Others are caused by bad people, or are the consequences of stupid actions. A lot of bad things happen when we get squeezed by the inflexible laws of nature. Most of the time it's not God's fault when bad things happen to good people.

How then do we salvage our faith in a God who is stripped of his power? Kushner tells us to cling to a belief in his innate goodness. Forgive the world for not being perfect. Forgive God for not making it better. Reach out to hurting people and bring them comfort. Go on living in spite of suffering. Redeem affliction by imposing a positive spin on it. If the play is badly written, rescript it for a better ending.

Kushner's redefined God neither causes nor prevents tragedies. He only helps by bringing people into our lives to comfort us. The good news is that God is not responsible when bad things happen. The bad news is that he is uninvolved and impotent. The really bad news is that prayer doesn't bring supernatural aid. It only provides a measure of peace for the hurting. Kushner is left at his son's grave with this confession:

"I can worship a God who hates suffering, but
cannot eliminate it, more readily than I can worship
a God who chooses to make children suffer and die
for whatever exalted reason." (page 134)

He stands in stark contrast to Job whose ten children were crushed to death in a cyclone. This grief-stricken father tore his robe, shaved his head in frenzied agony, and then visited the graveyard. In that place of unspeakable sorrow, he managed to worship God as both all-powerful and all-good in a praise song for the ages:

"Naked I came from my mother's womb,
and naked I will depart.
The Lord gave and the Lord has taken away,
may the name of the Lord be praised."

—Job 1:21

We might hope that Kushner's radical revision of Job's God brought some comfort to him, as well as those who read his book. But what good is comfort that deprives us of the only true Comforter? The supreme irony is that this grieving father's commentary on Job ultimately abandoned the very God who revealed himself so gloriously to that ancient sufferer.

The purpose of this book is not to debate Kushner's take on God. We deeply sympathize with him. Can there be any pain worse than losing a child? We do not want to be like Job's comforters, piously dispensing cookie-cutter formulas to Rabbi Kushner or anyone else who wrestles with the mysteries of human suffering.

May I do one act of love every day of my life

We recognize that answers come easily when one is not sitting on the ash heap of affliction. It is quite another thing if you are covered with boils, having lost everything precious. The same furnace of affliction that forges the steel of great faith can also melt it down to almost nothing.

In Job's debate with his comforters, there are moments when his theology is breathtakingly inspiring. At other times, his outbursts border on the sacrilegious. Anyone who has gone through a season of suffering will confess to times of intense faith followed by utter despair. Faith can be a roller-coaster ride. There are moments when Job's tortured observations differ little from Kushner's unorthodox conclusions.

Don't look for "one-size-fits-all" answers to ash heap questions. Job didn't find them. Neither did Rabbi Kushner. Nor will you find them in this book. Kushner's Torah says, "The secret things belong to the LORD our God..." (Deuteronomy 29:29) God does not choose to reveal everything to his puzzled children. He can be infuriatingly silent when we are most desperate to hear him speak. This too is a mystery.

Yet, one thing is certain: seasons of suffering are inevitable. Job's friend, Eliphaz observed, "Man is born to trouble as surely as sparks fly upward." (Job 5:7) Everyone will be called to play some part in a tragedy. A few of us will be typecast in such a role. As we go from struggle to struggle, we will wonder why others seem to get a bed of roses while we wear the thorns.

St. Paul limped across center stage, enduring excruciating pain for more than fourteen years. All the time, a demon hammered him with fists of fury. Few people have endured more pain for a longer time than Paul. This apostle repeatedly pleaded with God to rewrite the script of his life.

Almost every time he came into the spotlight, Paul was booed off the stage. He couldn't remember how many times the audience turned into a lynch mob. His critics wrote scathing reviews of his work. He often stood alone, abandoned by his best friends and vilified by those he loved most. Everyone who has ever spent time on the ash heap of affliction knows that it can be the loneliest place on earth.

St. Paul must have asked the same hard questions posed by Rabbi Kushner, Job, and maybe even you. Yet, like ancient Job, he found something far better than comforting answers when he discovered the God of all comfort. This God redeemed his afflictions. The ash heap of suffering showed Paul what it revealed to Job: God is as all good as he is all powerful.

St. Paul didn't get the final answer to why bad things happen to good people, but he did sing the praise song of Job. It has become the anthem of the afflicted:

> "Oh, the depths of the riches and the wisdom
> and knowledge of God!
> How unsearchable his judgment, and his paths
> beyond tracing out.
> Who has known the mind of the Lord?
> Or who has been his counselor?
> Who has ever given to God, that God
> should repay him?
> For from him and through him
> and to him are all things.
> To him is the glory forever! Amen."

—Romans 11:33-36

What allowed St. Paul to redeem his afflictions? An answer is tucked away in an epistle that he wrote to a First Century church in Ephesus. In this ancient letter, the apostle introduces us to a place unfamiliar to most Christians. I call it The Theater of Angels. The purpose of this book is to take us to that place so that our afflictions might be redeemed too.

In The Theater of Angels we won't find all the answers, but we may well discover our significance in the grand drama of the ages. In this theater we will gaze on the manifold wisdom and glory of the God of all comfort. We might even come to think of the ash heap of affliction as one of life's most redemptive places. If our peek into The Theater of Angels causes us to sing the praise song of Job and St. Paul, then this little book will have found its worth.

STORIES
SET IN STONE

A STUDY GUIDE

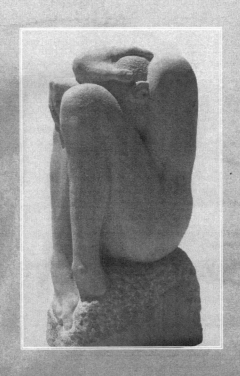

[handwritten margin note: Everything in heaven & on praises sing]

When Christ entered Jerusalem, his disciples filled the air with praise. Religious killjoys told Jesus to shut them up. He replied, "If they keep quiet, the very stones will cry out." (Luke 19:40) If everything was created to give God glory, surely rocks must cry out his praise too.

The Master Sculpture takes us raw and uncut from the rubble of this earth and chisels a masterpiece. Unlike inanimate stone, we feel the pain of the hammer, chisel, and file. Job suffers excruciating pain as he is shaped on the ash heap.

Artist Claudia Lauster's story connects to Job's, and is reflected in her sculpture. In her finished work, Job is less than four feet tall, carved out of a stone block. Yet, if he were to stand up, he would tower seven feet high. Suffering constricts Job into a box. Kushner had God neatly packed in his box of Jewish orthodoxy. After his son died, he stuffed the Most High into a new box of revised theology, as did Job and his comforters. But, when we reduce God to a box, we constrict ourselves even more. Here are questions to ponder and share with a small group as you connect Job's story to your own.

1. Oscar Wilde complained that the world is a stage, but the play is badly cast. Who do you think writes the lines and sets the plotlines of our lives? Is it God, ourselves, others, brute nature, or time and chance?

     [handwritten: All of the above, but mostly God.]

2. How would you respond to Rabbi Kushner's arguments that God cannot be all good and all powerful at the same time? Are we reduced to an either/or answer: *either* God is powerful and perverse *or* he is good but not in control?

3. Does Job 1:21 give a both/and answer: God is *both* powerful *and* good at the same time? How about St. Paul's famous words in Romans 8:28?

4. Why does God allow good people to suffer? Consider these verses: Genesis 3:16-19; Romans 8:22&24; Romans 6:23. Conversely, why does he allow the wicked to prosper? Think about Matthew 5:43-48.

He must allow wickedness to exist in order that there be a choice for goodness. This unfortunately means that some people are victims

_____

_____

_____

_____

5.   Many people think that it is unfair for good people to suffer. What
     do these verses say about our goodness: Psalm 53:3, Mark 10:18;
     Romans 3:10-18?

_____

_____

_____

_____

_____

6.   Deuteronomy 29:29 says that God doesn't reveal to us "the secret
     things that belong only to him." What baffles you most about
     human suffering? Why do you think that God hides so many
     mysteries from us?

_____

_____

_____

_____

_____

7.   Do you think that it is possible that, if we could find the answers
     and turn them into faith formulas, we would put our trust in them

instead of putting faith in God? Look at the last part of Deuteronomy 29:29. Has he revealed enough to satisfy you?

8. What is the difference between finding answers that comfort and the God who comforts?

9. Do you put God in a box? If so, what are you going to about it?

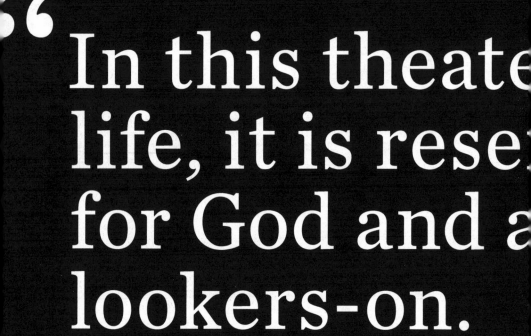

"In this theate[r] [of]
life, it is rese[rved]
for God and a[ngels to be]
lookers-on.

of man's

ved only

ngels to be

"

Pythagoras

Setting the Stage

THE THEATER OF ANGELS

IT WAS THE MUSICAL EXTRAVAGANZA of the season. Ignacy Jan Paderewski was performing at Carnegie Hall. In the audience that evening was a little boy who had been dragged to the concert by his mother in hopes that the legendary Paderewski might inspire him to practice his piano lessons more diligently.

As they waited for the concert to begin, the boy wiggled out of his seat and slipped down the aisle, irresistibly drawn to the Steinway on the stage. He climbed up and sat down at the piano. After placing trembling fingers on the keys, he began to play *Chopsticks*. A hush fell over the hall. Then the crème de la crème of society's elite turned into a snarling, screaming mob.

> "What's that child doing up there?"
> "Where's the brat's mother?"
> "Somebody get him away from that piano!"
> "Hey kid, get off the stage!"

Paralyzed by fear, the kid continued to bang out *Chopsticks*. Paderewski heard the uproar from back stage and rushed to the edge of the curtain. From there, the maestro watched the Carnegie Hall mob bully the boy. He angrily strode across the stage, encircled his arms around the petrified lad, positioned his fingers on the keyboard alongside the boy's, and began to improvise a countermelody to harmonize with and enhance *Chopsticks*. Paderewski kept whispering in the youngster's ear,

"Don't quit now."

"Keep on playing, kid."

"Whatever else you do, don't stop!"

MY STORY

I know exactly how that boy felt. My childhood was spent listening to people scream at me, "Hey kid, get off the stage!" It all started with my mother looking for love in all the wrong places. She found herself pregnant as a young teenager. I was the unplanned, unwanted, and unnamed baby. The identity of my biological father remains a mystery to this day.

Later my birth mother hooked a husband, an airman at the local Air Force base outside our town. They moved from Bangor, Maine to Eastern Washington where I was raised until age twelve. Her new husband was mostly gone on tours of duty, so my mother again looked for love in all the wrong places. Her nights were usually spent in sleazy taverns. Over the next half decade, she gave birth to five more children. No one can vouch for sure who their fathers were either.

She was infamous in our little town for sitting nine-months pregnant on a bar stool at seven o'clock in the evening. Fifteen minutes later, her labor pains began. Another barfly drove her to the hospital where she quickly gave birth to a girl. She handed the newborn to her friend and snarled, "You take the little snot, I don't want her." She was back on her bar stool by 9:30 that same evening. Meanwhile, I was the six-year-old back at the garage apartment taking care of my baby brothers and sisters, sometimes for days on end while my mother was out on a drunken binge.

One night, while mom was at the tavern, our little apartment caught fire. My sister Kim and I barely dragged our younger siblings out before raging flames gutted the place. I still bear scars from that inferno, along with the nagging question of how the authorities could miss the fact that a passel of kids was abused, abandoned, and living on the edge of disaster.

It was worse when our mother came home. Often she brought a boozing boyfriend with her, and involved me in their sex games. One night, a drunken lout sodomized me while she giggled. A day of reckoning came when her husband arrived home from overseas and saw our filth and squalor. He beat my mother with a belt until she fled from the house. The police came that evening, and we were all parceled out to temporary foster homes. Unfortunately, most of these foster parents were drinking buddies from the saloons my mother frequented.

My sister Kim and I were placed in the home of two drunkards. The man of the house beat his wife unmercifully during his frequent bouts of drunkenness. One night I pulled him off my little sister when he passed out after sexually abusing her. We often cowered in the corner when he went on his rampages. Later, he beat his wife to death with a hammer.

After that, we were dumped into the Washington State foster

care system. Mom promised that she would come back to get us. I never saw her again.

The foster system was a revolving door. We would just start to feel secure in a home, and then be reshuffled to another. In one home we ate out of dog dishes. In others, we were hardly fed at all.

When I was a nine-year-old, Wayne told me that I was his special boy, and he wanted to adopt me. A few weeks later, the case worker took us away to another home. I never saw Wayne again.

My biggest shame as a child was wetting the bed. I did so until I was almost 13 years old. Foster parents tried everything to break me of the habit: scolding, pleading, shaming, and finally beatings. Every night I pleaded, "God, please keep me from wetting the bed." The next morning the sheets would be wet again. It was as if God was mocking a little boy's prayers. In the morning, I would carefully pull the covers over the urine-soaked sheets, hoping that my "dirty nasty" wouldn't be discovered. At bedtime, I would crawl between rancid and damp sheets, praying again that this night would be different than all the others. It never was.

Washing day would inevitably reveal the soiled sheets and stained mattress. One foster mother finally had enough. She painted in bold black strokes across a big square of cardboard,

THIS BOY STILL WETS THE BED

She hung that cardboard sign on a rope around my neck and forced me to stand on the front porch while my classmates walked by on their way to school. This tactic didn't stop my bedwetting, but it *did* fill me with deep humiliation. That public shaming sums up my childhood. After that, I was teased unmercifully. Almost everyone called me Bobby Bedwetter.

A rare bright spot in my young childhood was the summer that I turned twelve. All six of us siblings were in the same little town, four of us together in a foster home. That idyllic season ended when Joe and Barden were adopted. As their new parent's drove away with them, I ran after their car screaming, "Come back, come back!" I can still remember their tear-stained faces looking at me through the rear window. When the car disappeared over the horizon, I threw myself facedown in a field beside the road and shook with sobbing until my body ached. Then I rose with dirt-streaked face, shook my fist at the skies, and yelled, "If there is a God, I hate you! I hate you!" I never saw my brothers again.

I built walls around my heart to protect it from hurt. A state psychologist wrote that I was a pre-teen with the sociability of a four-year-old. He assessed that I was incapable of giving or receiving love. I was still wetting the bed every night. Having been shuffled through so many homes, I had no sense of family or personal identity. A sixth grade teacher wrote on my report card, "This boy needs to be institutionalized, or he will never amount to anything." Rejection and loneliness can constrict us into a tiny box that is almost impossible to escape.

Who would have guessed that little Bobby would grow up to amount to something special? The God that I hated proved that he loved me more than I could ever imagine. But I will save that part of my story for the final scene in The Theater of Angels.

Just know for now that the ash heap of affliction is not unknown to me. In the years before and since my adoption by Arnold and Mary Petterson, I have often rubbed the ashes of broken dreams into the oozing sores of pain and sorrow.

Though Jesus, time and therapy have healed most of my

hurts, a severely dysfunctional childhood is not easily escaped. It has affected my marriage, ministry and mind. The English writer P.G. Wodehouse was right when he penned, "The boy is the father of the man." More than fifty years later, the old wolves in the cellar of my soul still rise from a long sleep to howl again at the most inconvenient times.

It was during an ash heap season that I discovered The Theater of Angels. In that theater of unending dramas I have watched stories of fellow sufferers played out on center stage. There are personal favorites to which I return often: Joseph, Moses, King David, and St. Paul. But I most often revisit the story of Job. When everyone seems to be screaming at me, "Hey kid, get off the stage," I find the courage to press forward from what happened so long ago in that mysterious land of Uz.

WHAT ABOUT YOUR STORY?

I suspect that you have your own story to tell. Like all of us, there are those times that you feel like you can barely bang out that beginner's piano piece, *Chopsticks*. It seems like the whole world is shouting at you, "Hey kid, get off the stage!"

Even the most heroic saints have experienced these moments. After his entire nation yelled at him to get off the stage, an Old Testament prophet lamented, "Why did I ever come forth from the womb to look on trouble and sorrow, so that my days have been spent in shame." (Jeremiah 20:18) Imagine a prophet of God wishing that he had been aborted. The prophet Elijah even begged God to kill him. St. Paul came close to a mental breakdown. Jesus wanted to die in the Garden of Gethsemane rather than face the horrors of the cross the next day.

Maybe you've not sunk quite that low, but I'll bet you've

had some days when you were so far down that you had to look up to see bottom. I'm guessing that you've sat on more than one ash heap of suffering. Live long enough, and you will discover that there's another season of tribulation just around the next corner. If you've ever felt like jumping off the stage, you are in good company.

I would like to invite you to accompany me to this showing in The Theater of Angels. As I confessed to you earlier, it's my personal favorite. I hope that you will be more than a spectator. I think that you will get the most out of Job's story by getting caught up in it. I like what American theologian Frederick Buechner wrote about stories:

> "At the deepest level the story of any one of us is
> the story of all of us. We have the same dreams,
> the same doubts, the same fears of the night."

Make Job's story yours too. You might just discover some life principles that will transform your own afflictions. Like Job, you might even become the hero of your own epic. Before the curtain rises on his blockbuster drama, please allow me to show you around the Theater of Angels.

THE ANGELS ARE WATCHING

The most fundamental thing you need to know about this theater is that there is a realm unseen by the naked eye. In this other dimension, a fantastic array of angels move undetected on silent wings. This invisible world is as real as the one we touch with our senses. Scripture calls it "the heavenly realms."

When the soldiers of an ancient Syrian warlord surrounded

the house of Elisha, the prophet's servant was hysterical with fear. Elisha prayed, "Open his eyes, LORD, that he may see." (2 Kings 6:17) The God of heaven opened the servant's eyes, and he saw fiery chariots filled with fire angels surrounding the Syrians. Rarely do these celestials show themselves. But there are times when the curtain is pulled back to allow mere mortals to peek into another world so awesome that even cynics are seized with terror and wonder.

St. Paul once peered into this other dimension. He saw sights and secrets that he was forbidden to divulge. But he was able to reveal one thing: The Theater of Angels. This is what he writes to Christians in the ancient city of Ephesus:

> "His intent was that now, through the church, the manifold wisdom of God should be made known to the rulers and authorities in the heavenly realms, according to his eternal purpose which he accomplished in Christ Jesus our Lord."
>
> —*Ephesians 3:10&11*

Paul was writing to Christians who were as frightened as Elisha's servant. Many were Jewish converts who had been disowned by their families and thrown out of synagogues when they embraced Jesus. Most were Gentile slaves. Some of these converts were destined to face lions in the arena. Surely the world was yelling at them to get off the stage. Maybe they asked the same question that haunted Rabbi Kushner at the grave of his son: "Why do bad things happen to good people?"

Paul doesn't answer all their questions, but he does offer comfort from the heavenly realms: angels are watching, and our suffering transforms them. Let's unpack these astonishing words in Ephesians 3:10&11.

SETTING THE STAGE

St. Paul is speaking the language of the theater. The arts were as significant to the First Century as they are in our media-saturated age. Every city had a playhouse with a troupe of actors. Ephesus was the Broadway of the Greco-Roman world. Her grand amphitheater sat proudly above the city in its crown position. In this mecca of entertainment, great spectacles wowed sold-out theaters. But nothing sold tickets like ravenous beasts devouring Christian martyrs on blood-soaked sands.

No Christian ever wanted to play center stage in the Ephesian amphitheater. We can hardly imagine the shame that those martyrs felt when they were led out of darkened tunnels into the hot glare of an Ephesian sun to the jeers of blood-thirsty spectators. Could there be a worse exit from life's stage than to be torn apart by beasts, and then what's left of your mangled corpse scooped off the sand while crowds hoot in derision?

But St. Paul wants us to ignore the catcalls of the audience. He asks us to shrug off the rotten reviews of the critics. The lions that prowl about us are only bit players in a larger drama. In the light of eternity, it matters little what we look like after the beasts have done their worst. You and I have far bigger parts to play before an infinitely more significant audience. It's the cosmic role of a lifetime on center stage in The Theater of Angels. Let's now see how Paul's letter to the Ephesians sets the stage, and what our part is in this epic drama:

The Playwright

Ephesians 3:10 begins with these key words: *"His* intent..."
God does everything with clear intention. Verse eleven calls it
"...his eternal purpose..." Because it is eternal, his purpose never
changes. God does not make up the story as he goes along. He
wrote the script of our lives well before he created the cosmos.
Our history is really *His* Story. Nothing is meaningless. No
experience is insignificant. No failure is wasted. No sin is
irredeemable. When the last scene has been played out,
our story will be seamless in its perfection despite all of
our botched lines and missed cues.

Sometimes, when we look at the chaos in our world, we
wonder if anyone is in charge. Postmodern culture views God as
the producer and director of a historical drama that goes something like this: the play opens with a garden scene. The leading
lady, Eve, steps on the leading man's toes. This causes Adam to
trip over a piece of scenery, which leads to a chain reaction of
props being knocked over. Sets have been toppling like dominos
ever since. Meanwhile, God scurries back and forth behind the
scenes, wringing his hands and shouting directions to actors and
stagehands. But no one pays attention.

Lines have been revised and rewritten in a frantic attempt
to fix the story. But all that remains is a gory mess of fallen
curtains, broken sets, and scattered pages of original script no
longer relevant. God sits alone in the rubble of a darkened and
deserted stage, his original paradise gone up in smoke. The
actors audition for roles elsewhere. The audience has left to
find other gods, diversions, and entertainments. Only a handful
of orthodox believers linger in an increasingly musty theater,

holding stubbornly to the delusion that their religious fairy tales will one day experience a revival.

St. Paul would vehemently disagree with such pessimism. Even in the chaos of global terrorism, economic woes, ecological disasters, and disintegrating moralities, God is still in charge. When St. John's world seemed to be falling apart, the doorway to heaven was thrown open to him. Nothing in his apocalypse rivals the first thing he saw: "...there was before me a throne in heaven with someone sitting on it..." (Revelation 4:2) Someone is in charge! A King sits secure on his throne, calmly watching the drama of redemption play out exactly as he planned it before the beginning of time. When the final curtain falls on the glorious conclusion to *His* Story, everything will make as much sense to us as it does to him now.

The Players

Who are the players on center stage, acting out this drama? Look again at verse ten: "His intent was that now through *the church...*" The true church is made up of individuals who have committed their lives to Jesus. It matters little whether we are great virtuosos or can only bang out *Chopsticks*. If we belong to Christ, he has written a part for us to play on center stage. Every line of our script is power-packed with eternal significance because he wrote it for us.

The Plot

What does the Playwright want to show through his church? St. Paul continues in verse ten: "His intent was that now, through the church, *the manifold wisdom of God might be made known...*" Savor that word manifold. It means that God's wisdom has many layers, dimensions, and facets. No matter how many layers we peel back, some secrets are too deeply hidden to be uncovered. Deuteronomy 29:29 says, "The secret things belong to the LORD our God."

Ephesians 3:9 adds that there are mysteries "...kept hidden in God..." Like our first parents, we desperately want to eat the fruit from "the tree of the knowledge of good and evil" so that our eyes might be opened. The tag line of a supermarket tabloid captures our obsession: "Inquiring minds want to know." God's ways have exhausted sages, tormented sufferers, and baffled saints. Even the angels are at a loss to comprehend the things known only to God. Yet St. Paul makes an astounding statement: your brief time on history's stage reveals something of God's inscrutable wisdom.

The Audience

If all the world is a stage, and we are the players who reveal God's wisdom, who then watches his production? Ephesians 3:10 goes on, "His intent was that now through the church, the manifold wisdom of God should be made known *to the rulers and authorities in the heavenly realms.*" When Paul uses the phrase heavenly realms, he is speaking of the invisible spirit world. In Ephesians 6:12, he identifies the rulers and authorities as angelic beings—the devils of hell and angels of heaven.

Having written a script for his church, God summons fallen angels and holy celestials to gather at The Theater of Angels. There they learn something of his glorious wisdom from *us.* Even during the mundane, silly, or absurd times of our lives, the angels are studying us intently. They pick up our throwaway moments and sift through them like priceless treasures. In our loneliest times, when it seems that God and everyone else has forgotten us, the angels are watching.

These angelic beings have seen the face of God. Yet the Apostle Paul audaciously claims that, when they watch us, they see something of his wisdom that they never see when they look directly at God. This too is a mystery. We may not understand it, but we can accept it because the Bible says it. If we seize this truth, we will never look at life the same way.

What's Paul's Point?

Remember, St. Paul is writing to a suffering church in Ephesus. He wants them to be encouraged by the fact that the angels will never see more of God's wisdom than when they watch us suffer. Angels learn more from martyrs who sing songs of praise in bloody arenas than they do from comfortable saints singing hymns in churches. When the crowd is booing our feeble performance, yet we refuse to get off the stage, we show far more of God's glory than if we were playing like a maestro to thunderous applause. Job shows the angels much more while suffering on a heap of ashes then he does when he is spouting a rich man's prayers in his stately mansion.

If we can only plunk out *Chopsticks*, it matters little what the highbrows at Carnegie Hall think or say. We must keep on playing because the Master will come in due time. He will put his nail-scarred hands next to our trembling fingers and play a countermelody that harmonizes with and enhances our *Chopsticks*.

More than that, he will turn it into a grand symphony in The Theater of Angels. But this will be no improvisation on his part. Every note of it was written with loving care before the first star ever spangled the night skies.

He asks only one thing of you and me: "Keep on playing, kid. Whatever else you do, don't stop now!" If we listen closely, we might even hear galaxies of heaven's angels beating wings in thunderous applause, or devils gnashing their teeth as they see God's glorious wisdom revealed in the weakness of humans they diabolically despise.

On Center Stage At The Theater of Angels

My ash heap afflictions are being wonderfully redeemed by putting into practice what I've learned at The Theater of Angels. Yours can be too. That's why I'm inviting you to join me as my special guest for another showing of Job's epic drama in The Theater of Angels.

Let's go quickly and grab the seats reserved for us. There's no time to waste. The curtain is about to rise on one of my favorite stories. It has repeatedly sustained me in more ash heap moments than I dare to remember. There are villains to boo and heroes to cheer. Plot lines will take our emotions on a roller coaster ride. Grab a box of tissues. We just might shed a few tears. But the ending is profoundly redemptive and rip-roaringly triumphant.

If you stay with me to the very end, neither of us may ever approach life the same way again.

STORIES
SET IN STONE

A STUDY GUIDE

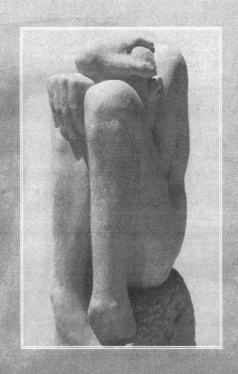

Of all the questions in life, these torment most: Why? Why me? Why this? Why now? Even Jesus screamed, "My God, My God, *why* have you forsaken me?" Claudia captures inner torment in Job's posture on the ash heap. His head is between curled up legs. A massive left hand holds it down. This is the protective hand. His right hand grips a leg as if holding himself back until he discovers answers. His feet are twisted and toes dig into the ashes, holding on to what is left of his ruined life.

Yet, in the inward struggle to find answers, Job is even more constricted. In searching for God's answers he has yet to find his Comforter. Let's use the following questions for personal reflection and then share them together with others who will help us expand our perspectives.

1. Do you ever feel like that little boy playing *Chopsticks*? Can you think of some experiences when you felt like jumping off the stage? How does it make you feel that great faith heroes have felt the same way? Look at Job 3:11-13, 1 Kings 19:4, Jeremiah 20:18, Matthew 26:38-42, and 2 Corinthians 12:1ff.

    _____

    _____

    _____

    _____

    _____

    _____

2. Look again at the story in 2 Kings 6. What do you think you would see if you could pull back the curtain and really peer into the heavenly realms? What would the room look like right now?

3. What do these verses teach us about angels touching our lives?
    1 Kings 19:4-6, 2 Kings 6:17, Psalms 78:25&46, Mark 5:9, Ephesians
    3:10&11, Ephesians 6:10-12, and Hebrews 13:2

4. How would your life change if you really believed that your time
    on life's stage was really playing to watching angels instead of only
    the watching world?

    I would be more careful about
    caring for the souls of people +
    about always doing the right
    thing.

5.   Where is God when our world is upside down? Consider Revelation 4:2, Hebrews 1:8, Daniel 7:9, Isaiah 6:1&66:1. How do these verses make you feel?

6.   If God wants to make his wisdom known through you, when are you best able to show it: when you are at your strongest in the good times or weakest in the tough times? For St. Paul's perspective look at 1 Corinthians 1:26-31 and 2 Corinthians 12:9&10.

7.   What are the angels looking for in 1 Peter 1:10-12? How does that make you feel about yourself?

_____

_____

8. How did you react to the idea that Jesus has written a master symphony to harmonize with and enhance your *Chopsticks*?

_____

_____

_____

_____

_____

_____

Does it give you confidence that he doesn't improvise to make up for your mistakes?

_____

_____

_____

_____

What difference would that make in how you view your past sins and mistakes? It might help to go back and look at Romans 8:28 again.

_____

_____

_____

_____

" I call the boo
from all the t
it, one of the
things ever w
a pen.

of Job, apart

eories about

randest

itten with

"

Thomas Carlyle

Act One: Scene One

THE MAN FROM UZ

THE LIGHTS DIM AND THE curtain rises in The Theater of Angels. The narrator begins the first scene with one of the most familiar opening lines in literature: "In the Land of Uz there lived a man whose name was Job."

THE SETTING: THE LAND OF UZ

This drama is immediately shrouded in mystery. We know that Dorothy found Oz somewhere over the rainbow, but no one knows for sure where Uz was. Scholars think that it may have been on the Persian Gulf, near the city of Ur where Abraham was born. Perhaps the man from Ur heard the story about the man from Uz, and it was passed down by generations of his family until it found its way into Jewish Scriptures.

The fact that Uz can be found on no maps reminds us that the places important to God are sometimes wide spots on the road to nowhere. Heaven's attention is often focused on those that we ignore: shepherds, carpenters, poor widows, and beggars. Many of us spend lives in obscure places like Uz. People take little notice of us. Even if they do, they won't long remember us after we are gone. But if we could peer into the heavenly realms, we might see row upon row of angels on the edges of their seats, watching us intently. Even out-of-the-way places like Uz take center stage in The Theater of Angels.

THE HERO: A MAN CALLED JOB

Uz is important because Job lived there. No place is unimportant, if you live there. No story is trivial, if it is yours. No role is minor, if God calls you to play it. None of your afflictions is meaningless if it teaches the watching angels something about the manifold wisdom of our Lord. Uz may not be significant, but Job is. And so are you!

A hush falls over the angelic audience as Job strides onto center stage. Catch your breath. This is not only Job's story, it is yours too. Only a few lines sketch his character, but they are the hooks on which the rest of the story hangs.

> "This man was blameless and upright: he feared God and shunned evil. He had seven sons and three daughters, and he owned seven thousand sheep, three thousand camels, five hundred yoke of oxen and five hundred donkeys, and a large number of servants. He was the greatest man among all the people of the east."
>
> *—Job 1:1-3*

Righteous Job

Job was "blameless and upright." This is amazing when you consider that he lived among pagan people. Some say that his name was *Bo Ya*, from an ancient Semitic language that originated somewhere in the Middle East. Job was not Jewish. Yet God may have known this man from Uz before he called Abraham to leave Ur. The name *Bo Ya* most likely means "one who is hated or counted as an enemy."

Other scholars say that his Semitic name was *Jaab*, which means "to love or desire." His parents gave him that birth name to announce to the whole world that their baby boy greatly delighted them. During later nights of agony on the ash heap, it must have been difficult for him to feel like *Jaab*, the one desired by God. More likely, he thought of himself as *Bo Ya*, the one God hates as an enemy.

Centuries later the Jews adopted this Gentile as a faith hero and changed his name to *Jobé*, which has since been Anglicized to Job. His story proves that God reaches out beyond his covenant family to transform people from every tongue, tribe, and nation. Job lived long before Moses brought the Law down from Mt. Sinai. He didn't own a Bible. He wasn't a child of Abraham. Yet the Holy Spirit moved across desert sands until he found a pagan Gentile named *Jaab* in the land of Uz, and then transformed him into a spiritual giant.

Whatever moniker you hang on Job, you must at least call him good. The word "blameless" means that no one could find fault with him. The word "upright" simply means that he walked tall and cast a big shadow. He could stride ramrod straight and unashamed into any room, and then look everyone straight in the eye, because he had nothing to hide.

As the Uzites watched his wealth pile high and his progeny grow to ten children, they most likely judged him by the theology of their day: he was blessed because he had pleased God, and his family grew because children are a heritage from the Lord.

He also "shunned evil." British Lord, John Acton wrote, "Great men are seldom good men." Lord Acton famously observed, "Power corrupts, and absolute power corrupts absolutely." When CBS news anchor Dan Rather asked President Bill Clinton why he had an affair with White House intern Monica Lewinski, the world's most powerful man replied, "I did it because I could." We should stand in awe that the accumulation of prosperity, prestige, and power didn't corrupt Job. The more he amassed, the faster he ran from sin.

Job shunned evil because he "feared the Lord." He knew full well that our God is a consuming fire. Though he lived some 2,000 years before St. Paul, he grasped this apostle's timeless warning: "Do not be deceived. God cannot be mocked. A man reaps what he sows." (Galatians 6:7) Job understood that we can avoid a lot of bad harvests if we fear God's judgment on sin. Surely he lived out the words that King Solomon penned a thousand years later: "The fear of the Lord is the beginning of wisdom." (Proverbs 1:7)

His respect for God's holiness extended to his family. He adored his kids, but didn't pamper them. Yet it's hard for children of affluence to avoid the corrupting effects of privilege. In the opening lines of Job's story, we read that his sons took turns hosting parties in their homes, inviting their sisters to join their bouts of drinking and feasting. (Job 1:4)

We don't know what happened at those weekend bashes, but enough reports came back to worry their daddy. He took the spiritual condition of his trust fund babies seriously. Later, after they were crushed to death in a tornado, he cried out, "What I feared has come upon me; what I dreaded has happened to me." (Job 3:25) Job did not fear God without reason. He knew that sin has consequences, even for the ten children that he desperately loved. Though they repeatedly broke his heart, this godly dad never failed to take remedial action:

> "When a period of feasting had run its course,
> Job would make arrangements for them to be
> purified. Early in the morning he would sacrifice
> a burnt offering for each of them, thinking,
> 'Perhaps my children have sinned and cursed
> God in their hearts.'"
>
> —*Job 1:5*

Righteous Job took his unrighteous children to God's throne of grace. Ten of his best animals were sacrificed. Their blood was sprinkled on Job's kids for their purification. He did this because he trusted in the blood sacrifice to atone for sin. How did a man living in a pagan culture know to do this?

Did he know that his burnt offerings prefigured a true and better Lamb of God who would shed his blood? When he put those sacrificed animals in the fire, did he know that the Lamb of God would even descend into the flames of hell to pay for the sins of God's unrighteous sons and daughters? How much Job knew is yet another mystery tucked away in this story. But surely he had a faint inkling of the grace of God that would be wondrously displayed on a Roman cross outside Jerusalem some 2,000 years later.

Job was not a saved man because he was a good man. Rather, God declared Job to be righteous by imputing to him the righteousness of the only Lamb who can save. Any goodness that he possessed came because the Redeemer's sanctifying grace transformed him. Listen to what God says to the devil:

> "Have you considered my servant Job? There is no one on earth like him; he is blameless and upright, a man who fears God and shuns evil."
>
> —Job 1:8

It's one thing for the watching world to say that you are blameless and upright. It's quite another for God to declare it. Again, Job's goodness wasn't generated by his own flesh efforts. He was born just as sinful as the rest of us, a fact proven by the waywardness of his children. As the old saying goes, "The apple doesn't fall far from the tree." He later confessed, "Even if I were innocent, my mouth would condemn me; if I were blameless, it would pronounce me guilty." (Job 9:20)

Yet, he had a deep and personal assurance that he was purified by the blood sacrifice of the Lamb. Later, when he doubted his standing with God, he said of the Most High, "Though he slay me, yet I will hope in him." (Job 13:15) Job's eternal hope rested in his Redeemer's goodness, and not his own. He was a trophy of God's grace.

Rich Job

His wealth was also a gift of God's grace. Later, when he lost everything, Job fell prostrate on the graves of his children and cried out, "Naked I came from my mother's womb, and naked I will depart. The LORD gave and the LORD has taken away..."

(Job 1:21) He understand what few of us grasp: we come into this earth with nothing and we will leave the same way. Whatever life gives in between is a temporary loan drawn from the bank of God's grace. No one was ever lavished with more of heaven's generosity than Job. Like an accountant, the Holy Spirit writes in the ledger of Scripture:

> "He had seven sons and three daughters, and he owned seven thousand sheep, three thousand camels, five hundred yoke of oxen and five hundred donkeys, and a large number of servants. He was the greatest man among all the peoples of the East."
>
> *—Job 1:3*

Notice the repetition of tens: ten children, ten thousand head of sheep and camels, ten thousand oxen and donkeys. In Hebrew numerology, the number ten and its multiples is symbolic of completeness or fullness. When Psalm 50:10 says that God owns the cattle on a thousand hills, it is literally saying that our Lord owns *all* the cattle in the world. This repetition of tens is Scripture's way of saying that Job had it all. He lacked nothing. Had *Forbes* listed the richest men of his day, Job would have topped the list. He was the Bill Gates of 2000 BC. Verse three sums up his charmed life: "He was the greatest."

It is astounding that he was rich and righteous at the same time. Jesus said, "It is easier for a camel to go through the eye of a needle than for someone who is rich to enter the kingdom of God." (Matthew 19:24) Yet Job was the rarest of people who are both great and good. He didn't sacrifice his spirituality to become successful, nor did he pursue his career at the expense of his family. He was one of those precious few who reached the highest rung of the ladder of success while still earning the applause of heaven.

Respected Job

Read again those words that sum up his success: "He was the greatest man among all the people of the East." (Job 1:3) That word "greatest" not only refers to his wealth, but also to his stature. No one was more esteemed than Job. His legendary wisdom caused top leaders to seek his counsel. When he walked into a room, everyone stood up out of respect. When he spoke, they all listened. His righteousness and riches added up to a third thing that made life pleasant for Job: the reverence of people and the admiration of God.

Later, when he lost his children, wealth, and health, it was the loss of respect that tormented him most. When he was covered with boils, scabs, worms, and stinking to the high heavens, Job hid himself away in shame. Men who used to swoon when he looked their way now mocked him as a loser. He lamented, "God has made me a byword to everyone, a man in whose face people spit." (Job 17:6) People may forfeit riches, and even doubt their own righteousness, but to lose the respect of others is the cruelest blow of all.

THE SUM TOTAL OF A MAN

Three pleasant words sum up Job's life: righteous, rich, and respected. People seldom possess all three at the same time. Most will sacrifice righteousness to attain riches. They will crawl to the top rungs of the ladder of success in ways that cause them to lose the respect of God and people. A Fortune 500 CEO said, "I spent my whole life climbing to the top of the ladder of success, only to discover that it was leaning against the wrong wall." But Job was able to hold on to his soul as he created wealth and earned the respect of others. Every story needs a hero. Few fit the bill like the man from Uz.

Maybe that's why, some 4,000 years later, his monumental collapse still causes us to ask, "Why could so many bad things happen to such a good person?" This is the sort of tension that creates the drama in every good story, especially Job's starring role in The Theater of Angels.

You will want to watch what happens to Job in the next scene, because his story is really about you and me. Just as Job had to spend his not-so-fleeting hour in the limelight, so there are ash heap roles aplenty for you and me yet to play on center stage.

STORIES
SET IN STONE

A STUDY GUIDE

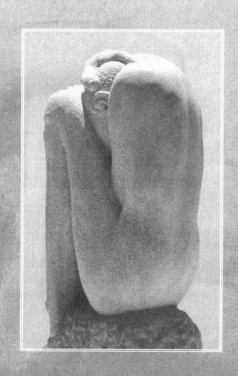

Claudia's sculpture of Job sits in a courtyard of the Covenant Church of Naples, Florida | PCA on a patio surrounded by gardens and framed by church doors. From a distance, Job might be praying a righteous man's prayers at church. But a closer look shows that he is in despair on an ash heap of suffering. We are reminded that righteousness is not enough to protect us from the proverb of Eliphaz: "Man is born for trouble as surely as the sparks fly upward." Jesus said to his disciples, "In this world, you will have trouble." Shallow theology says that faith rewards us with blessings. Yet bad things happen to good people, even as the wicked prosper. Faith more likely sees us through the bad times so that we become better able to handle the blessings in the good times. Let's discuss together some things that we have learned from Job's good times.

1. Are there any insignificant places or little people? Think of places where God has turned the wheel of history: Uz, Ur, the back side of the Sinai Desert, Bethlehem, Nazareth, and the Island of Patmos. Can you think of other out-of-the-way places where little babies were born in obscurity to change the world?

   _____

   _____

   _____

   _____

   _____

   _____

2. The watching world was convinced that Job was blessed because he was a good man. If this is true, what about the lament of Solomon

in Ecclesiastes 5:8-17, or the questions posed in Jeremiah 12:1, Psalm 73:3, or Job 21:7?

3. If Job was declared righteous because he was good, where did his kids get the DNA that led to their sinfulness that required purification? Look again at Job 1:4&5. Look also at his confession in Job 9:20. What then does it mean for God to declare someone righteous as he did in Job 1:8?

4. What do we learn from the blood sacrifices in Job 1:5? How do you suppose a man coming from a pagan culture, well before Moses, figured this out? See Romans 1:18-20, Romans 2:25-29, 1 Corinthians 2:10&12:3.

_____
_____
_____
_____

5.   What do we learn about wealth from Job 1:20-22? Why is it so hard
     to be both rich and godly at the same time? Look at the words of
     Matthew 29:24.

_____
_____
_____
_____
_____

6.   What earns the respect of the world? Is it possible to earn God's
     approval and the watching world's respect at the same time? Look
     at Job 1 and try to figure out how Job managed both.

_____
_____
_____
_____
_____

7.   Do you agree that it's harder to lose the respect of others than
     wealth, health, and loved ones? Look at the bitterness of Job 17:6.
     Look at his whole speech. Have you ever felt like Job?

8.   Having watched Job's charmed life, what makes him most impressive to you? What do you learn from his successful life?

9.   What does his sudden fall from the top rungs of the ladder of success tell you about your own situation? If you still have time to ponder and discuss, look at Ecclesiastes 5:18-20.

" There's only
hero and eve
that the devil
to be the goo

oom for one
yone knows
doesn't get
guy. "

Jim Hill

Act One: Scene Two

THE LION OF HELL

GREAT DRAMA IS ALWAYS A tension between good and evil, ruin and redemption, hero and villain, hopelessness and rescue. So it is with The Theater of Angels. But Job's unendingly pleasant life makes for a vanilla story. Evil, darkness, and villains are the spice of drama. We quickly lose interest in Paradise until Adam and Eve take those first steps toward the forbidden fruit. Excitement rises when the Serpent slithers out of the shadows. We may boo the villain, but he does add sizzle to the show.

Multiple Oscar winning actor Christoph Waltz, who has made a career out of playing villains, once said, "You need a villain. If you don't have a villain, the good guy can go home." Legendary film director, Alfred Hitchcock observed, "The more successful the villain, the more successful the movie."

This has significant implications for our lives. We love the drama that the villain brings to other people's stories, but we hope that he keeps his distance from us. Like Job, we prefer unending success. But we are shortsighted to opt only for the safe life. We might as well wish for a spin on the merry-go-round. It's harmless and predictable, but nauseatingly boring as it goes round and round.

God has designed life to be a white knuckle, heart-in-your-throat roller-coaster ride. We never know what's around the next curve or over the next rise in this ride of sheer drop-offs, anticipation, panic, and exhilaration. The rewards of the roller-coaster are so much greater. Merry-go-rounds are for children who are too easily scared or satisfied. Who, but the most timid of adults, would be content to go in endless circles on a painted pony when they can ride the wild horses to high adventure?

THE DRAMA IN THE DANGER

Meaning is found in the ups and downs of roller-coaster living. If we didn't suffer pain, we could never savor pleasure. Spring is rendered more glorious by the bleakness of winter. Grace is made amazing because of our wretchedness. If we never had problems, we wouldn't discover that God can solve them. Without a villain, we would never need a hero. Life is so much richer when it becomes riskier.

We live in an age that is obsessed with peace and security. We work feverishly to build fail-safe systems that insulate us from anxiety and pain. We create political correctness to shield ourselves from hearing unpleasant realities, and fastidiously avoid commitments that might lead to broken hearts. But the Bible offers a radically different worldview. When God made the Garden of Eden, he could have built a fail-safe system. But a risk-free paradise would have been a merry-go-round paradise. Everyone in The Theater of Angels would have fallen asleep watching perpetual reruns of Happily Ever After.

Instead, God planted a forbidden fruit tree at the epicenter of Paradise. He didn't make the illicit fruit drab and unappealing, but created it to be titillating to the senses. God brought instant drama to Paradise when he planted that tree.

When he created humans, he didn't make them automatons, programmed robotically to love and obey him. He gave them free will to make decisions for themselves. Then he heightened the drama by telling them that their choices had consequences. If they ate that fruit they would unleash a firestorm of sin, suffering, and death. Then he further upped the ante by allowing the Serpent to have access to Adam and Eve, just as he later gave the snake access to Job, and sometimes allows him to slither into our lives and wreck havoc.

That tree was like a ticking time bomb in the middle of Paradise. Even though we've seen the reruns a thousand times, we still lean forward in our seats when Eve reaches for the forbidden fruit. God didn't stack the odds in his favor to guarantee the perfect outcome. The Garden of Eden was Paradise precisely because it could be lost.

From the beginning God has called us to adventurous living. We never know what will happen when we turn to the next page of our life's script. For Job, things couldn't be sweeter. But paradise can be lost in the twinkling of an eye. The page turns, the villain appears, and everything changes in The Theater of Angels.

EMISSARIES FROM HELL
Even while Job is at the altar offering sacrifices for his children,

angelic visitors are approaching heaven's throne. At exactly the same time he is pleading for God's mercy, events are taking place that will strip him of everything he holds dear in life. The merry-go-round is about to come to a jarring stop. The devil is going to take Job on a roller-coaster ride from hell, and God will stamp the ticket. The plot thickens as we read,

> "One day the angels came to present themselves before the Lord, and Satan came with them."
>
> —Job 1:6

Who are these visitors to heaven? The King James Version of the Bible best translates the original Hebrew by identifying them as "the sons of God." We first see this phrase "sons of God" in the chaotic days before Noah's flood: "The sons of God saw the daughters of men, that they were beautiful; they took wives for themselves of all whom they chose." (Genesis 6:2) Later, the Bible uses this term "sons of God" to refer to angels. Who were these angels who copulated with humans? They could only be fallen angels, for holy celestials wouldn't engage in such perversions.

According to the Genesis account, during the Pre-Flood Age these copulating celestials produced a race of giants who were half-human and half-angel. They were known as the Nephilim. The Jewish apocryphal book of Enoch called these fallen angels the Watchers. (I Enoch 6-36) It goes on to say that when their Nephilim offspring died, they lived on as demons.

If the book of Enoch is true, demons are to be distinguished from the angels who fell from heaven in Lucifer's rebellion. Fallen angels have bodies; their demon progeny are disembodied spirits. They roam the earth looking for the bodies of earth's creatures to possess. Like their fallen angel parents, demon offspring do the bidding of Lucifer. These half-breed spirits also find a seat at The Theater of Angels.

We might be tempted to dismiss this fantastic teaching because the writings of Enoch are part of the Jewish Apocrypha. But we cannot ignore it because the New Testament book of Jude quotes from Enoch when it calls those fallen angels who had sexual intercourse with women, "...those who did not keep their proper place..." (Jude 6) The writer of Jude goes on to associate these fallen angels with the perversions of Sodom and Gomorrah. Both involve sexual relations outside the created order set by God: angels with humans and sex between people of the same gender.

Suffice it to say, fallen angels and demons are two different kinds of being, although both are numbered among what St. Paul calls "...rulers and authorities in heavenly realms..." (Ephesians 3:10)

Somehow a precious few in the line of Adam managed to avoid intermarriage with humans whose DNA might have been tainted with that of fallen angels. Certainly, Noah's family did not carry this seed of perversion. Some have speculated that God had to destroy the earth with a flood, lest the bloodline of the coming Messiah (or any of us) become tainted with the genetic code of fallen angels or their Nephilim offspring.

Now back to the "sons of God" who appear out of nowhere in the story of Job. Though they have been cast out of heaven, fallen angels are sometimes summoned to the throne of God. They may gnash their teeth in anguish, but they must come and bow their knee to their Creator when he calls them.

THE THEATER OF ANGELS

These dark outcasts of heaven often appear there alongside the angels of light. The Old Testament prophet Michiah had a curious revelation in 2 Chronicles 18. In his vision, God decided to put a lying spirit in the mouth of a false prophet to destroy a wicked king. God asked who would go for him as that lying spirit. Several angels eagerly stepped forward. God sent one of them on his way to put lies in the mouth of the nefarious prophet.

Who were these angels who enthusiastically volunteered to spin a web of deception to destroy a king? They could not be holy angels, for such celestials do not tell lies. They must have been fallen angels like "the sons of God" who now appear in the story of Job. Fallen angels and their demon offspring are so consumed with evil that they will even do God's bidding if it gives them a chance to fulfill their insatiable desire to destroy.

If God will unleash a lying spirit to put deceptive words in a false prophet's mouth, we should not be surprised that he might even give permission to a destroying spirit to do his worst to a righteous person like Job. This devil angel or demon spirit will surely fly from God's presence with diabolical delight to do its worst, but God will use what it does to bring about his best.

SATAN UNMASKED

Standing among these emissaries from the dark kingdom is the puppet master of fallen angels and demons. Job 1:6 says, "...and Satan came with them." He is aptly named. His moniker comes from the Hebrew verb *sata*, which means to turn away, swerve away, or fall away. Later the verb morphed into the noun *Satan*, which came to mean "the Adversary." In Medieval times, the

Church took the sound of the first Hebrew letter in the word *Satan* and turned it into our word *sin*. Ancient Jews slightly changed *Satan* to *Shatan*, which means "to urinate." Such was the disgust that they had for Satan.

Satan goes by thirty-three different names in the Bible. The one most often used is *devil*, which means the Accuser or the Slanderer. He was originally called *Lucifer*, the Shining One. Other popular names for this prince of fallen angels are *Beelzebub*, the Lord of the Flies; *Apollyon*, the Destroyer; *Belial*, the Worthless One; the Dragon and the Serpent. There are other names that are equally chilling.

We shouldn't fixate on him or be overly fearful of his power. C.S. Lewis delivered this warning in his witty commentary on demons, *The Screwtape Letters*:

> "There are two equal and opposite errors into
> which our race can fall about the devils. One is to
> disbelieve in their existence. The other is to believe,
> and to feel an excessive and unhealthy interest
> in them. They themselves are equally pleased by
> both errors and hail a materialist or a magician
> with the same delight."

Martin Luther said, "The best way to fight the devil is to mock him." The half-brother of Jesus wrote, "Resist the devil and he will flee from you." (James 4:7) Yet, he doesn't possess his ominous names without reason. Vast is the number of his victims. In his classic book, *The Art of Warfare*, Sun Tzu stated that the first rule of warfare is to know your enemy. If we are going to triumph over this formidable foe, we should know his story.

The Angel of Light

He was once God's most glorious angel. The prophet Isaiah cried out, "How you have fallen from heaven, morning star, son of the dawn!" (Isaiah 14:12) The Hebrew word for dawn is *shachar*, which literally means "Bringer of Light." This was the title sometimes given to worship leaders in ancient Israel. Some scholars postulate that Lucifer may have been the Director of Worship in heaven. If that is the case, then he had the most exalted angelic position. There is nothing more pleasing to God than to be praised by those he has created for his glory. Listen to this description of Lucifer by the Prophet Ezekiel:

> "You were the model of perfection, full of wisdom and perfect in beauty...every precious stone adorned you...your settings and mountings were made of gold; on the day you were created they were prepared... You were on the holy mount of God; you walked among the fiery stones. You were blameless in all your ways from the day you were created until wickedness was found in you."
> —Ezekiel 28:12ff.

No angel was more beautiful than Lucifer. He was the model of perfection; the gold standard of God's creative genius. When Ezekiel writes that he "walked among the fiery stones," he is telling us that Lucifer was once numbered among the Seraphim or Fire Angels, the highest order of angelic beings. Isaiah calls him "Son of the Light Bringer." Before God brought light and energy into the cosmic void, his creative genius birthed Lucifer as the premier angel of light. It's no wonder that St. Paul warns us to beware of his coming to us as an angel of light. (2 Corinthians 11:14)

Ezekiel 28:15 says of Lucifer, "You were blameless in all your ways until wickedness was found in you." Just as God created a risky Paradise by giving the first humans the choice to do good or evil, so he designed heaven with the same risk. Lucifer and all the other angels were given free will to decide whether to serve God or rebel against him.

Lurking behind the glory of the Son of Light Bringer was the demon seed of pride. When did this secret pride explode into a fire angel's naked rebellion? Insights from Ezekiel and Isaiah may well reveal the shocking answer to this ancient mystery.

Guardian of Eden

We have traditionally assumed that Lucifer rebelled against God before the Garden of Eden was created, and was hurled down to earth *before* he slithered into Paradise to tempt Adam and Eve. But Ezekiel 28:13 says, "You were in Eden, the garden of God." According to Ezekiel's narrative, he was in the Garden before "wickedness was found in him." Ezekiel 28:14 says, "You were anointed as a guardian angel, for so I ordained you." God set apart his greatest archangels to guard the crown jewel of his creation, our first parents.

Ezekiel 28:14 says that before Adam and Eve fell into sin, Lucifer still "walked on the holy mount." He was still counted among the "fiery stones" or Seraphim Fire Angels. God must have seen the pride that was eating away at his most beautiful angel. Yet he gave him the charge to guard Adam and Eve. God never plays it safe. He didn't do it when he sent his Only Begotten Son to die on a cruel cross. Neither will he play it safe with Job or the rest of Adam's offspring, including you and me.

Could the following be the dynamic that changed everything in the Garden? The angels were the apex of God's creative genius, and Lucifer was the loftiest of them all. Then God created the first humans. Psalm 8:5 says that God made them "...a little lower than the angels." As Adam rose from the dust of the earth, this puny little clay creature must have been singularly unimpressive to the Son of Light Bringer. Adam was made from dirt. Eve was fashioned from the DNA of one of the dirt man's ribs. But Lucifer was created from heaven's fire. He was dazzling light, and they were red clay. He soared on fiery wings through the heights of heaven while they crawled across the face of the dust from which they came.

Yet those clay creatures had something that the Son of Light Bringer could never possess. God had breathed his spiritual essence into them. His very image was encoded in their DNA. The Creator walked in easy intimacy with them in their garden, and even called them his children. As the Son of Light Bringer watched, jealousy rose like unholy bile. Imagine his humiliation. As the loftiest of the Fire Angels, he was now forced to serve as a ministering angel to the naked and clueless clay creatures!

Ezekiel 28:16 says, "You were filled with violence." Envy is the smoldering tinder of inner rage that eventually explodes in violence against others. Filled with fury, Lucifer determined to destroy the clay creatures and seize control of the cosmos.

Falling from Heaven

Ezekiel continues to chronicle the downward spiral of the Son of Light Bringer. "Your heart became proud on account of your beauty, and you corrupted your wisdom because of your splendor." (Ezekiel 28:17) Pride gave birth to the rebellion described by yet another Old Testament prophet:

> "You said in your heart, 'I will ascend to heaven; I will raise my throne above the stars of God; I will sit enthroned on the mount of assembly; on the utmost heights of the sacred mountain. I will ascend above the clouds; I will make myself like the Most High."
>
> —Isaiah 14:13&14

Lucifer's conceit was to ascend to the dizzying heights of heaven and sit on its throne. He was angry at the way God was running things, so he decided to wrest control from him. This has profound application for Job and every one of us. God seldom runs his universe the way you and I might wish. We want to indulge ourselves in the lap of luxury, but he puts us on an ash heap of suffering. We want to grow old enjoying our children, but he makes us stand at their gravesite. Rabbi Kushner could never accept that God would allow his son to suffer with progeria and die at age fourteen. He found it even harder to tolerate his own grief in the aftermath of that tragedy. The list of things that we don't like in life is long. Yet, when we've had a gutful and try to take control of our marriage, children, church, or anything else that frustrates, we can be sure that Lucifer's seed germinates within discontented souls.

The third chapter of Genesis reveals the diabolical scheme. The Son of Light Bringer violated his trust as protector of Adam and Eve by morphing into a deadly serpent. We ought to be profoundly moved by the difference between Lucifer and God: when he wanted to destroy us, this angry angel became a snake; when a loving God saved us, he became a man.

It was so easy for this crafty fire angel to deceive the naïve clay people. The great rebellion that began in the Garden of Eden quickly spread. Lucifer flew on blazing wings of fire to seduce one third of the angels. Revelation 12:7 declares, "There was war in heaven." God's loyal angels fought back, and the fury of this angelic war shook the cosmos. We can only imagine the power and fury unleashed in history's first war.

O How the Mighty Have Fallen

No one knows how long that clash of the titans lasted, but the loyalist angels triumphed. Isaiah exults in Lucifer's fate:

> "All your pomp has been brought down to the grave...how you have fallen from heaven, O morning star...you have been cast down to earth."
>
> —Isaiah 14:11&12

God shouts triumphantly, "I drove you in disgrace from the mount of God...and I expelled you, O guardian angel from among the fiery stones." (Ezekiel 28:16) Daniel Defoe's little book, *The History of the Devil*, captures Lucifer's fate in some of literature's most vivid prose:

"Satan has been banished to be a wanderer, without fixed abode or space allowed for him to rest the soles of his feet. He inhabits the vast wasteland of liquid air, and will someday be cast into a bottomless pit. He has no home, has no future. His hell is to wander in insatiable loneliness and rage."

Yet the book of Job now records him back in heaven, summoned by royal command. God asks, "Where have you come from, Satan?" (Job 1:7) God knows where he has been, but he takes pleasure in rubbing the fallen angel's nose in his own disgrace. Satan's proud heart rebels at answering the question, but he has no other choice. So he hisses back, "From roaming the earth, going back and forth in it." (Job 1:7)

Heaven smirks. The rebel who wanted to sit on heaven's lofty throne now wanders like a vagabond through liquid grey wastelands. He has no home and no future. He who was created out of the purest fires of heaven is now destined for the blackest fires of hell. Every time he comes before the throne that he covets for his own, he is forced to answer that same question: "Where have you come from, Satan?" It is so nauseatingly humbling to be forced to repeat the horrifying reality of his damnation, "From roaming throughout the earth, going back and forth in it."

His time is short. The doomsday clock is ticking down to that day when Lucifer, together with all his fallen angels and demons, will be cast into what Jesus called "outer darkness." Imagine Lucifer's fury. Ezekiel tells us that he is covered with the rarest of precious jewels. Those adornments are his pride. But jewels need light to make them sparkle. When the doors of hell are shut up forever, not a molecule of light will filter through to reflect the jeweled splendor of the fallen Son of Light Bringer. Imagine the agony of this proudest of all God's creatures when his former radiance is snuffed out forever.

Yet, he is still the lion of hell on the prowl. His ultimate doom is sure, but he cannot forgive or forget his humiliation. Christ may have crushed his head at the cross, but a wounded and cornered beast is the most dangerous. Job will discover that when the lion sinks his teeth into everything he possesses and shakes it to smithereens.

But before we get to that, the plot must thicken a bit more in The Theater of Angels. Take a deep breath. The next scene is a doozy.

STORIES
SET IN STONE

A STUDY GUIDE

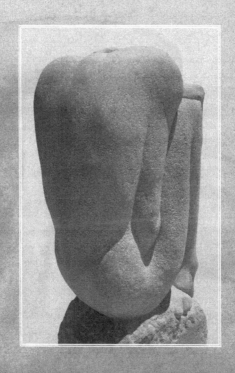

From almost every perspective, Claudia's sculpture captures the destructive power of Lucifer. In it we are stunned by the dark angel's hatred of God's beloved clay creatures. It is fitting that this clay creature from Uz is captured in stone. Satan's attacks can turn the softest souls into stone cold hardness. Job's body is contorted. His head is weighed down and hangs between his legs. Look at how his back is twisted in knots of agony and misshapen by the rampage of Satan. Luther was right when he said that our Enemy is armed with cruel hate that has no equal on earth. We must never forget that.

Yet, even as Claudia chiseled and shaped a block of stone into Job's ash heap suffering, she did it with profound love for the man and his story. In the same way, even as our Adversary tries to decimate and destroy us, a loving God is using that hatred as his chisel, hammer, and file to reshape us into his masterpiece. Let's meditate on dialogue about these mysteries.

1. Do you prefer the merry-go-round or roller-coaster, a painted wooden pony or wild horses? Why do you think that God created a high risk paradise? Look again at Genesis 2&3

2. If you knew that, at exactly the same time you were praying, Satan was asking to sift you, what difference would that make in your prayers? See Luke 22:31-33&39-36.

_____

_____

_____

_____

_____

_____

_____

3.   What do you make of God using Satan or other demons to do his work? See Luke 22:31, 2 Chronicles 18:18-21, 2 Corinthians 12:7&8. What do you think that these verses have to do with our Lord's Prayer: "...lead us not into temptation; deliver us from the Evil One..."?

_____

_____

_____

_____

_____

_____

4.   How do we avoid the twin dangers mentioned by C.S. Lewis: to disbelieve in angels' existence or to be overly excessive about them? Do you agree with Luther that we best combat him by making fun of him? How do we resist him? See James 4:7, I Peter 5:8&9, Ephesians 6:10 ff., 2 Corinthians 2:9-11.

_____

_____

_____

_____

_____

_____

5.   Was this the first time you heard this interpretation of Lucifer's fall? Take time to read and reflect on Ezekiel 28, Isaiah 14, Revelation 12, and Genesis 3 in the way they are woven together to show Satan's great conspiracy and rebellion.

_____

_____

_____

_____

_____

6.   What did you think of Daniel Defoe's description of Satan's punishment in his _The History of the Devil_? Do you see the reminder of judgment in God's questions and the anger of defeat in the devil's answers in Job 1:7 & 2:2?

_____

_____

_____

_____

_____

7.   What was your reaction to Ezekiel 28:13 and the author's suggestion that the outer darkness of hell would snuff out forever the radiance of Lucifer's jeweled pride? What does that teach us about hell? What does it say about us?

_____

_____

_____

_____

_____

_____

8.   Ezekiel 28:14 speaks of the King of Tyre and Isaiah 14:9-11 speaks
     of the kings of the earth. Why do scholars see these kings as one
     in the same with Satan? See in Matthew 16:23 where Jesus calls
     Peter Satan. When might Jesus call us Satan?

_____

_____

_____

_____

_____

9.   Why is Satan on the prowl to destroy us? See 1 Peter 5:8&9,
     John 10:10, Ephesians 6:12&13. What does this mean for you
     in practical terms?

_____

_____

_____

_____

_____

_____

" There is a big
between bein
crafty. The fo
attribute of G
latter that of

difference

g wise and

mer is an

od, and the

Satan. "

Michael Bassey Johnson

Act One: Scene Three

THE DEVIL'S WAGER

MANY OF US REMEMBER THAT blockbuster film of 1973, *The Sting*. It won seven Oscars, including Best Picture. The plot of this caper film was complicated, but it kept audiences sitting on the edge of their seats through several plot twists right up to its delightful and suspenseful ending.

The plotline can be summed up in a few words: during the Great Depression in 1936, two professional grifters played by Robert Redford and Paul Newman set up a vicious mob boss, using his own greed to lure him into a trap. The sting works. They con the mobster out of a fortune, and are on their way before he can figure out that he's been taken.

God is no grifter. He has never done anything dishonest. But he has written a part for Job to play on center stage in The Theater of Angels. To accomplish this, he has planned the sting of the ages. Just as Redford and Newman's characters used the mobster's greed to lure him into a trap, God will use Satan's craftiness to get him to go after Job.

But Job is only an unwitting player in the bigger sting being played on Satan. God always has bigger things in mind than what we see with limited vision. Job's time on center stage in The Theater of Angels will point to Jerusalem 2,000 years later and touch our lives today.

THE SET-UP

French poet, Anatole France, wrote tongue-in-cheek, "We have never heard the devil's side of the story, God writes all the books." Certainly, God has written the book on Satan. Let's watch how he sets him up. "Where have you come from?" asks God in Job 1:7. "From roaming throughout the earth, going back and forth on it," replies the devil. As we have already seen, the Creator is reminding Satan of his punishment for rebellion. He now roams the earth as a vagabond

God also knows something else about this lord of the fallen angels. When Satan replies, "From roaming throughout the earth," he is also describing his predatory activity. We hear an echo of Satan's words in St. Peter's warning:

> "Be alert and of sober mind. Your enemy the
> devil prowls around like a roaring lion looking
> for someone to devour."
>
> *—1 Peter 5:8*

The same Lucifer, who hated the clay creatures in the Garden of Eden, equally despises their sons and daughters. They possess everything that he can never have. Even the worst of these humans bear God's image and are loved by him. Though they have all sinned against the Lord of heaven, they have a shot at redemption that is beyond the devil's reach. Even atheists, agnostics, and worshippers of false gods enjoy God's common grace. But all of that is shut up to fallen angels. In *The Inferno*, John Connolly captures some of the pathos in Satan's relentless and destructive prowl:

> "He was the source of all that was bad in men and women, but had none of the greatness, and none of the grace of which human beings are capable, so that only by corrupting them was his own pain diminished, and thus his existence made more tolerable."

Satan especially hates a particular tribe of humans. When St. Peter says, "...your enemy, the devil..." he is speaking to Christians. Most of Adam and Eve's sons and daughters are still lost. But many have been found and brought home. These prodigals have put their trust in the Lamb who purified them with his shed blood. They are now the King's kids and heirs to the heaven that's no longer home to fallen angels. They may still be children of clay, but they walk this earth with the light of God shining brightly in and through them. Imagine the fury that this present reality must incite within the former Son of Light Bringer who now roams in the perpetual darkness of rage.

The one that St. Peter calls the lion will stalk God's children to the ends of the earth to devour them. If he can snuff out the light in a single clay saint, he will have struck a retaliatory blow against his Creator. The war that started in heaven still rages.

These redeemed clay people are the battlefields on which the conflict is waged. They are the Old Testament believers and New Testament Christians. Among them is a man called Job.

"Where have you come from, Satan?" asks God. The devil might as well have answered, "I've been roaming the earth looking for trophies of your grace to devour." God knows the inner violence that rages within his ancient adversary. He will flip that rage to display his manifold wisdom and grace to all who have gathered to watch a sting operation for the ages.

SETTING THE HOOK

Celestials of heaven and hell catch their breath. Whenever the Most High God and his ancient protagonist face off, the air is supercharged with tension. God poses a second question:

> "Have you considered my servant Job? There is no one on earth like him; he is blameless and upright, a man who fears God and shuns evil."
>
> *—Job 1:8*

The Hebrew word "considered" means to stare intently or study closely. Maybe Satan has only heard about Job in passing. Perhaps he has only taken a fleeting glance. It could be that he has never heard of Job at all. Remember, Lucifer is a finite creature. His terrible rage and frightening power cause us to exaggerate his capabilities. But he can never be like our Creator: ever present, all knowing or all powerful. There are now more than seven billion people on planet earth. Satan and his demons cannot possibly know them all. Consider yourself most fortunate if devils are ignorant of your existence. No sane person wants to attract the attention of the lio? pride of fallen angels, or his demon jackals.

Yet God points Job out to the devil. If the man from Uz were able to listen in on this conversation he might protest, "Creator, why are you exposing me to the enemy of the righteous? Is this any way to treat those who love you?"

Job would be even more furious if he could see God pointing out his sterling qualities to the devil lion: "...he is blameless and upright, a man who fears God and shuns evil." That is enough to ignite Satan's smoldering rage. But God further fans the bonfires of the devil's vanity: "There is no one on earth like him." The Creator is boasting that, of all the clay creatures that he has redeemed, Job is by far his finest trophy of grace.

It's delicious fun to watch God masterfully bait the hook (as long as your name isn't Job). The Most High knows that the lion of hell is roaming the earth in an unending quest to find his sheep and then devour them. And now he has pointed out the fattest and juiciest of his flock feasting on his sumptuous goodness down in the land of Uz.

The Serpent may be the craftiest creature of all, but God is the All Wise Creator. Wisdom trumps craftiness every time. God has set the bait, and dangled it enticingly before his greedy eyes. The Most High knows that violence will cause the lion of hell to leap for the bait.

The first reaction of any fair-minded person is to protest, "But Job is the bait!" This cosmic chess game between two old enemies may be heaven's sport, but it is monstrously unfair to make Job and his family pawns in that game. We could try to defend God by rationalizing that Job is God's servant, and servants exist to do the will of masters. But what master would employ his prerogatives and power to put his servant through a hellish nightmare just to score points against an old adversary?

Let's not jump to conclusions quite yet. This is The Theater of Angels. The drama of Job is full of plot twists and surprises waiting on the next page of the script. Who wants to read a book, go to a movie, or sit through a stage play that doesn't hold you in suspense until the end? What will Satan do with the bait? Will he devour Job and destroy God's work of grace? Will the all-powerful God prove himself to be all good? Can Job's afflictions be redeemed? What will you and I discover about ourselves and our own suffering? All this and more awaits those who are patient until the final curtain.

THE DEVIL'S WAGER

Satan takes a closer look at Job who dangles on the hook before him. But the crafty old lion is still wary of his Adversary. Skepticism sits moist on his beard as he growls back,

> "Does Job fear God for nothing? Have you not put a hedge around him and his household and everything he has? You have blessed the work of his hands so that his flocks and herds are spread throughout the land. But now stretch out your hand and strike everything he has, and he will surely curse you to your face."
>
> —*Job 1:9-11*

The fallen angel's retort is most cynical. Of course Job is righteous. It pays to serve God when he not only blesses you, but then puts an impregnable wall around all those riches so that you can't lose them. Who with half a brain would mess up a deal like that by biting the hand that feeds him?

Satan is asking a probing question that ought to challenge every child of God. Why do we serve the Lord? Is it for pure love, or do we do it for the goodies that he might send our way? The ancient Romans had an expression that is still used in political circles today, *quid pro quo*, which literally means "this for that." "If you scratch my back, I'll scratch yours." Too many folks have a Quid Pro Quo Faith that says, "If God blesses me, I will bless his name. If he doesn't, I will stop believing in him."

The old Serpent is as crafty today as he was when he slithered into the Garden of Eden. He knows that human nature is self-serving. He has identified and tagged the question that smolders in our hearts: "What's in it for me?" He knows how prone we are to bail out of relationships when our needs aren't being met. He's watched too many religious folk abandon faith and curse God when they lose that which is dear to them.

Of course there are exceptions to the rule. Everyday, heroic people keep on loving the unlovable and serving the ungrateful. They remain faithful in barren relationships, grind it out in unfruitful ministries, care for invalid spouses, love rebellious children, keep their word when others go back on theirs, and remain loyal to friends who suck the life out of them.

If you are one of these folk who refuses to live by the Law of Quid Pro Quo, may your tribe increase. You are a light shining in the darkness, and the salt that keeps our world from decaying. Don't stop now, even though times are tough and no one seems to notice or care. Remember, the angels are watching. You may not hear their applause, but they are cheering for you. You are one of heaven's heroes.

But Satan knows that only a precious few continue to love God and others when there seems to be no returns. The question that he poses about Job is really about us too. It is imperative that you and I answer this question:

> Will I still love and serve God even if he allows all that I hold precious to be stripped away, and leaves me with no tangible rewards for worshipping him?

Long ago I answered this question with the vow of an Old Testament warrior: "But as for me and my house, we will serve the Lord." (Joshua 24:15) That resolve has been tested on many ash heaps. My personal struggles compel me to give this warning: don't wait until you are on the ash heap of affliction to answer the question! Job had already settled the issue long before the devil showed up to wreck havoc in his life.

GOD TAKES THE CHALLENGE

Having set the hook, the Most High quickly responds: "Very well, then, everything he has is in your power, but on the man himself, do not lay a finger." (Job 1:10) God has set the hook and is reeling old Slewfoot in. The sting operation is off and running. But there are some important nuances in what God says to the devil. If we don't grasp them, we will miss the heart of this drama in The Theater of Angels.

1 God Never Punishes His Children

Satan challenges God to stretch out his hand of power and strike everything that he has lavished on the man from Uz. (Job 1:11) Instead, God gives the devil authority to strike everything that Job possesses. God will not do anything that is evil. The half-brother of Jesus wrote,

But god allows the temptation

> "When tempted, no one should say, 'God is tempting me.' For God cannot be tempted by evil, nor does he tempt anyone."
>
> —James 1:13

James goes on to say that God sends only good gifts from above. Our heavenly Father never strikes his children in anger. He may discipline those of us who belong to him, but he never punishes us. He has already exhausted his wrath on his Only Begotten Son who took our place at the whipping post. Here's how an Old Testament prophet describes Christ's crucifixion:

> "Surely he took up our pain and bore our suffering, yet we considered him punished by God, stricken by him, and afflicted. But he was pierced for our transgressions, he was crushed for our iniquities; the punishment that brought us peace was on him, and by his wounds we are healed...the Lord has laid on him the iniquity of us all."
>
> —Isaiah 53:4-6

When Jesus cried out from the cross, "It is finished," the punishment for all of our past, present, and future sins was taken care of forever! This is as true for Old Testament saints like Job *good point to always remember.*

as it is for New Testament Christians. For God to strike any of his redeemed children is unnecessary and redundant. For us to beat ourselves up when we sin, or others when they hurt us, is a repudiation of Christ's work. We are saying that he didn't suffer enough, so we have to take it upon ourselves to dish out more punishment. We might as well ask him to climb back up on the cross and finish what he already said was finished.

It took years for me to figure out this truth and apply it to my life. When my mother sexually abused me as a child, she would stroke my head afterwards and say, "You make mommy feel so good." I bought the lie that I was the one who caused her to do the things that made me feel dirty. When I was beaten, an angry foster parent would say, "Bad boy, you made me lose my temper." I grew up believing that bad things happened to me because I was bad. Later, I applied this to God. No matter how good things were, I always expected the "other shoe" to drop at any moment. I never asked why bad things happened to good people. I only knew that they happened to me because I was somehow *bad* people.

Maybe you've fallen into my trap. Like a Medieval monk, you flagellate yourself whenever you mess up. Lots of folk beat themselves up with negative self-talk. They assault others with demeaning talk. There is a sickness worse than spousal or child abuse: the abuser tells the victim, "You made me angry enough to beat you up," or "You led me on, so I raped (or, molested) you." It is double abuse when battered and bruised victims are left believing that it was their fault.

We are all quite capable of blaming ourselves when bad things happen. Religious folk are quick to believe that they are getting a well-deserved whipping by God. They actually think that a sermon is better when a hard-nosed preacher delivers

God's beating from the pulpit. If we aren't sure whether our trials and tribulations are God's punishment, others will be quick to suggest the distinct probability that it is. If they don't, the devil will be there to whisper condemnations in our ear. It's no wonder that St. John called him, "...the accuser of the brothers..." (Revelation 12:10)

The cross liberates us from such bizarre thinking. Before I could redeem my ash heap afflictions, I had to separate my experience with abusive earthly parents from my thinking about my heavenly Father. For me, this was a painstakingly long process (it is for everyone who was mistreated by parents). Yet I have come to embrace the wonderful doctrine of the cross. When Jesus said, "It is finished," no punishment remained for me, or anyone else who rests in God's grace. Dear friend, may I ask you also to face this question head on?

> Will I choose to see my trials and tribulations as the punishment of an angry God, or the discipline of a loving Father designed to make me a better person?

2 God Works Through Second Causes

Scripture gives this clear answer: God will work through evil-doers, and even your own sins and stupidities, to accomplish good. Though he will never lift a hand against his children, he will allow evil forces to do bad things to them for their ultimate good. He allowed Joseph's brothers to sell him into slavery so that he might eventually rise to become Prime Minister of Egypt and save fledgling Israel from starvation. God didn't put jealousy in the hearts of Joseph's brothers. He didn't whisper in their ears to sell the young man into slavery. Nor did God put it in the heart of Potiphar's evil wife to accuse him of rape so that he ended up in an Egyptian prison. Every step along the way evil people put Joseph into another bad place. But God used these bad places to transform this once-arrogant youth into a servant leader. Each step that evil people forced him to go down was just another rung up God's ladder to the throne of Egypt. In the end, Joseph was able to say to his brothers, "You intended to harm me, but God intended it for good to accomplish what is now being done, the saving of many lives." (Genesis 50:20)

Grasping this biblical doctrine of "second causes" was one of the greatest breakthroughs on my road to healing. When people hear my story, they often ask, "How did you learn to forgive and move on?" I don't use pious platitudes to wall-paper over evils that others have inflicted on me. Afflictions aren't redeemed through dishonesty, or by stuffing painful memories. We are often told, "Forgive and forget." Forgiveness doesn't require amnesia. Forgiveness means that those past hurts no longer wound, control, paralyze, or demand rage or revenge.

How did Joseph forgive? He didn't do it by pretending that evil didn't happen. He didn't excuse what his brothers did. He didn't trivialize his own pain. But he did recognize that their evil actions were used by a good God to bring about better things. I now rejoice in the excruciating pains of childhood and adulthood because God has been in them all, shaping and preparing me for glorious things that I could never experience or achieve without them. So here's another question that I often ask myself. Maybe you will find it helpful too:

> Will I count it all joy when trials and tribulations come, allowing them to make me *better* rather than *bitter*?

very very hard.

As one who has sat on my share of ash heaps, I can guarantee you that they don't necessarily get easier with time. I can assure you that, if you have settled the above question, you will only sink so far until you hit the solid bedrock truth that better days are ahead.

3 God Holds the Devil's Leash

There is never a moment when the Most High is not in control. To say that the God of Job's story is not all powerful is to misread or misrepresent the script. Satan understands this reality when he says, "Have you not put a hedge about him and his family and everything he has?" (Job 1:10) No force in the universe can harm us as long as God puts an impenetrable wall around us. Isaiah 54:17 promises, "No weapon formed against you shall prevail." Even when God allows Satan to go on a rampage, he sets strict parameters: "But on the man himself, do not lay a finger." (Job 1:10)

When Satan later gets another shot at Job, God allows him to harm his body, but he is not permitted to kill him. God is the final arbitrator of all things, especially death. King David says to God, "...all the days ordained for me were written in your book before one of them came to be." (Psalm 139:16) We never have to fear an uncertain future. St. Paul gave one of the greatest promises in Scripture: "For we know that in all things God works for the good of those who love him, who have been called according to his purpose." (Romans 8:28)

Christians often quote this verse. But it's one thing to say "Amen" to its sentiments; It's quite another to existentially believe it at the very core of your being. It has taken me years to believe that God always had my highest good at heart when the worst things were happening. I've had to overcome years of childhood conditioning in order to let go of fears. I think that's why I resonate with a line from the movie *Hope Floats*. It's lead character, played by actress Sandra Bullock, comes from a weirdly dysfunctional family, and it has messed up her thinking. In the final scene, she says, "Adulthood is spending the rest of your life getting over your childhood." I have answered this question repeatedly. Maybe you might like a go at it:

> Will I release my anxieties and fears to God, and rest in the fact that he controls all things for my ultimate good?

4 The All Powerful God is All Good Too

If God is in control, is he still good? Rabbi Harold Kushner says that we can't have it both ways. Either God is all powerful but perverse in setting Job up for suffering, or he is all good and unable to stop evil. Rabbi Kushner demands an *either/or* solution. Another Jewish rabbi, St. Paul, declares that it's a *both/and* deal. God is all powerful and all good at the same time. He writes in Romans 8:28, "...in all things God works..." He is in control of *all* things. They turn out "...according to his purpose." He is not only in control, he is powerfully so. At the same time, "...God works for the good..." What he powerfully accomplishes always achieves good for "those who love him and are called according to his purpose."

[handwritten margin note, left:] FREE WILL allows for evil.

[handwritten note, bottom:] his final purpose is GOOD but for now he must allow evil due to free will.

How this works out in Job's life is yet to be seen. The Playwright of heaven wants to keep us in suspense. The full answer will not come until the final scene of his story in The Theater of Angels.

But consider this for now: what if Job isn't as righteous as he seems? Is it possible that he still has room for personal growth? Could it be that his suffering in the refiner's fire will make him far better in the end?

What if the excruciating testing of his faith produces something far more precious than everything he loses? What if the end game in his life produces far more happiness for Job than he might have ever enjoyed without a season of suffering?

What if heaven is made better, and millions of people down through the ages are strengthened and encouraged by Job's triumph over tribulation? What if God's amazing grace is established beyond a shadow of doubt by what happens?

What if we see Christ's person and work, the abiding presence and power of the Holy Spirit, and the glory of God the Father more clearly in Job's tribulations and triumphs? Suppose we find redemption in our own afflictions and discover meaning in the sufferings of those we dearly love?

If all of these things could be shown to be true in Job's story, wouldn't it be possible to say that God is all powerful and all good at the same time?

There are so many questions to ponder, and so many answers yet to be found. But now it's time for an intermission. Dear friend, this is as good a moment as any to deal personally with questions that have been posed. The Theater of Angels always forces us to think deeply and act courageously. But right now we have some time to go off alone and do some personal business with ourselves and God.

Please return for Act Two. Then stick around for Act Three. You just might find the answers and help in The Theater of Angels that will change everything forever.

STORIES
SET IN STONE

A STUDY GUIDE

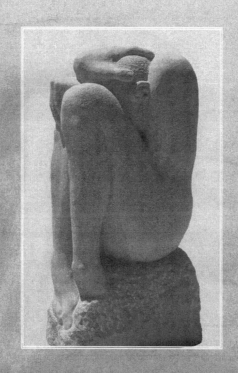

Job is not on the ash heap because of his wrongdoing. In fact, it is his very goodness that puts him there. C.S. Lewis said, "Why shouldn't the righteous suffer? They are the only ones who can handle it." The very phrase "handle it" comes from the word hand. Claudia brilliantly captures that. Notice the huge left hand over Job's head. Artists see the left as the female hand. It is associated with compassion. Claudia sees this as God's hand of empathy over Job's agony. It is attached to Job's arm that is weak and compressed, squeezed between legs that tighten in anguish. God's hand of grace and our arm of faith work together in partnership.

This wager between two ancient adversaries, using Job as the bait, spawn questions that cut at the heart of everything. Let's meditate and discuss these questions together.

1. If wisdom is an attribute of God and craftiness of Satan, what is the difference between the two? See God's wisdom: Job 12:12, Psalm 37:30, I Corinthians 1:25, Colossians 2:2&3, James 3:17, Romans 11:33-36. See craftiness: Job 5:13, Luke 20:23, 1 Corinthians 3:19, 2 Corinthians 4:2, and Ephesians 4:14.

2. How did you feel about God setting up Satan by using the man from Uz as the bait in Job 1:8? How would you feel if God used you as bait in a similar wager? Would this be fair?

_____

_____

_____

_____

_____

3. C.S. Lewis said, "Why shouldn't the righteous suffer? They are the only ones who can handle it." Do you agree with him? Do you think God would allow you to go through it if he knew you couldn't handle it? Look at 1 Corinthians 10:13. Is it possible to say that your suffering is a compliment from God?

_____

_____

_____

_____

_____

4. Look at Satan's argument in Job 1:9-11. What proves whether or not you have a Quid Pro Quo Faith? Look at Romans 8:31-39 versus 1 John 2:19.

_____

_____

_____

_____

_____

_____

5.   Have you settled the issue posed by Satan regarding Job: to serve God even if there are no rewards for your worship in this life? See Joshua 24:15, Job 13:5, Romans 9:3 & 12:1&2.

_____

_____

_____

_____

_____

_____

6.   Was the doctrine of second causes new to you? See Genesis 50:20, 2 Corinthians 12:7-10, James 1:2-4. Does this doctrine help you to forgive those who have hurt you (see Luke 23:34)? What does it mean to forgive and forget?

_____

_____

_____

_____

_____

_____

7.   What causes some to grow bitter while others grow better with their suffering? See Genesis 50:20, Luke 23:34, 2 Corinthians 12:7-10.

_____
_____
_____
_____
_____
_____

8.   Do you believe that God always holds the lion's leash (Job 1:2&2:6)?
     How can you release your fears and rest in him as all wise, all
     powerful and all good? Do you see all three of these attributes of
     God in Romans 8:28?

_____
_____
_____
_____
_____

9.   The author gave a list of reasons why God's initiating of this wager
     was a good thing. Do you agree with his reasons? Is there any you
     would add, or subtract? Do you think that you would be willing to
     undergo affliction for the same ultimate good?

_____
_____
_____
_____
_____

"Nothing more
baffles one w
trick and dup
straightforwa
integrity in a

completely
o is full of
city than
rd and simple
other. ”

Charles Caleb Colton

Act Two: Scene One

UNLEASHING THE LION

SATAN HAS BEEN UNLEASHED. ALL hell is about to break loose in the Land of Uz. Outside of Jesus' agonizing Good Friday, perhaps no one ever had a worse 24 hours than Job. Before it is over, a day of unimaginable catastrophes will stretch into months of unabated affliction. If you think that Job's story is too crazy to be true, you haven't met the Ugandan mother who laid twelve of her sons in the grave, all of them killed within days by Dictator Idi Amin's thugs. You didn't talk to the Florida woman whose son found out that he had terminal cancer the day before her grandson was diagnosed with leukemia and three days before she was told that she had Parkinson's disease. A week later her husband suffered a heart attack. Job's story is not beyond the possibility of human experience.

WHAT'S IT ALL ABOUT?

Almost everyone will say that the central question of Job's story is, "Why do the righteous suffer?" If that's the case, the story fails to deliver. We know more than the players in Job's drama because we've been made privy to the dialogue between God and Satan. They were left to figure things out for themselves. We also possess New Testament truths that Job and his friends never heard. But the loose ends of Job's story aren't neatly tied up for us either.

The greatest stories, plays, movies, and art force us to leave theaters and galleries haunted by questions not answered. They inspire conversation and debate. Jesus spoke in parables that produced more questions than answers. He often left his stories unfinished. A great story draws us in, compels us to make it our own, and then forces us to write our own endings. We may long for easy solutions and predictable plotlines, but we are made better by having to wrestle with the story. Perhaps that's why 19th Century Scottish philosopher Thomas Carlyle wrote, "I call the book of Job, apart from all the theories about it, the greatest thing ever written with a pen."

Job's story is not so much about why the righteous suffer as it is, "Will the righteous persevere?" Remember the devil's accusation: "Stretch out your hand and strike everything he has, and he will surely curse you to your face." (Job 1:11) This is a frontal attack on the integrity of Job's walk with God. Satan is saying that Job's commitment to righteousness is based on the Quid Pro Quo Law of "I'll serve God as long as he blesses me." This is the compelling drama in Job's story: once his riches and respect are stripped away, will his righteousness disintegrate in the face of disappointment?

Satan is also attacking the integrity of God's saving grace. He is saying that God can't keep those that he redeems. He challenges one of God's greatest guarantees in Holy Scriptures:

"If God is for us, who can be against us...Who shall
separate us from the love of Christ? Shall trouble
or hardship or persecution or famine or nakedness
or danger or sword?...No in all these things we are
more than conquerors through him who loved us.
For I am convinced that neither angels nor demons,
neither height nor depth, nor anything else in all
creation, will be able to separate us from the love
of God that is in Christ Jesus our Lord."

—Romans 8:31-39

Over the next months of his life, Job will experience every trial and tribulation listed by the Apostle Paul in the eighth chapter of Romans. This is the burning question for Job, and every one of us who ends up on the ash heap of affliction: will the love of God that is in Christ Jesus keep us secure and safe to the end?

INTEGRITY'S FIRST TEST

The day from hell dawns when a messenger bursts into Job's house with news that desert bandits have stolen his oxen and donkeys, and put his servants to the sword. (Job 1:14&15) This harbinger of doom is still spilling his guts when a second rushes into the room with more bad news that a firestorm has consumed his sheep and all their shepherds. (Job 1:16) Just when things couldn't seem to get worse, a third messenger breathlessly arrives to join the chorus of doom. Raiders have swept in to steal his camels and slaughter all of their keepers. In a matter of minutes, Job hears the shattering news that his financial empire has collapsed.

No human mind can process such a tsunami of bad news. Job stands there stunned and speechless. This series of catastrophes ought to shiver our timbers too. Life is fragile. All the things that we depend on for security are like the proverbial house of cards. A single event can cause our whole world to come crashing down. A sudden screech of brakes, a pain in the chest, a diagnosis from the doctor, and everything changes instantly. No one can predict when international events will spiral out of control, stock markets crash, terrorists attack, or an ecological disaster strikes. There are no fail-safe systems.

Our only hope is that God has put a hedge around us. But we can never know what's going on in the heavenly realms. On the night before Christ's crucifixion, Peter boasted that he would follow Jesus all the way to the cross. He confidently predicted that he would not fold under pressure like the other disciples. Jesus replied, "Simon, Simon, behold, Satan has asked that he might sift you as wheat." (Luke 22:31 *ASV*) That night God tore down the hedges that protected Peter, and allowed the lion of hell to go after him just as he went after Job. We should never assume that God wouldn't tear down our hedges if he thought that the sifting process would reveal our flaws and begin the process of reshaping us. He might even tear down the hedges in order to show watching angels and humans something of his amazing grace as it redeems our afflictions.

Back to Job's story. The woes brought by the first three messengers pale before the shattering news that comes from the last harbinger of doom. A tornado has crushed all ten of his children. (Job 1:18&19) This tragedy is made all the worse by the revelation that his trust fund babies were killed in the midst of one of those revelries that made their godly dad worry. He hadn't even had a chance to purify them with a blood sacrifice before they died. Job must wonder, "Did they have time to repent?"

The death of loved ones is so much more devastating if we aren't assured that we will see them in heaven someday.

The 19ᵗʰ Century English writer Samuel Richardson wrote, "Calamity is the test of integrity." Why bad things happen isn't as important as how we respond to them The devil is banking that Job's faith will collapse under the weight of these massive body blows. How much bad news can any person take without throwing in the towel? None of us could fault Job if he shook his fist at the heavens and cursed God.

A GRIEF OBSERVED

Make no mistake about it, Job is totally undone. He grieves loudly and long in Middle Eastern fashion. He slashes at his rich robes until they hang in tatters. He takes a razor to his head and beard until nothing is left but cuts and bruises. He screams in frenzied agony. Off stage his wife can be heard sobbing inconsolably. Job is not a stoic who stuffs his pain. Faith in God never calls us to accept heartache with a stiff upper lip, or hide swollen eyes behind a black veil of respectability. An old Yiddish proverb says, "Our tears rend the heavens." In a moment of grief, King David cried out to God, "...put my tears in your bottle; are they not in your book?" (Psalm 56:8 *ESV*)

Did Job know that God was collecting every one of his tear-drops like precious pearls and putting them in a bottle? Do you know that God prizes every tear that has ever trickled down your face? It's of inestimable comfort to know that each of our sorrows is recorded in God's memory book as his precious keepsake. If it breaks our heart to see our children weep when they are being disciplined or going through those heartaches that forge the steel of character, how much more will our pain move our heavenly

's heart, even when he rips down the hedges and allows
tions to flood in.

PRAISE AT THE GRAVE

King David wrote, "Weeping may stay for the night, but joy
comes in the morning." (Psalm 30:5) We don't know how long
Job wept, or how many nights he held his wife in his arms as
she sobbed in that deeper grief that can only be experienced
by a mother who loses her babies. Yet eventually he went out
by himself, fell prostrate on the ground, and burrowed his
head into the freshly dug dirt that covered his children's graves.
As barren winds blew across his desolate and empty estate, Job
did the unimaginable. He raised a face covered by the mud of
tears mingled with dirt, and worshipped the God who had torn
down the hedges and unleashed the lion:

> "Naked I came from my mother's womb, and naked
> I will depart. The Lord gave and the Lord has taken
> away; may the name of the Lord be praised."
>
> —Job 1:21

Right from the beginning, God gave his creatures choices.
Lucifer had a choice as to whether he would be satisfied to
guard the clay figures in the Garden, or become embittered
because he had to do that which he felt was beneath his dignity.
Adam and Eve had a choice to enjoy their orchard of delights, or
grouse in dissatisfaction until they took the one fruit that was
forbidden. Job too had a choice: he could allow his afflictions
to turn him bitter or make him better. He could praise God or
curse him. Each of us has the same choice when we are faced with

disappointments and heartaches. Indeed, the choices we make in our calamities are the greatest test of our integrity.

Job passes his first test with flying colors. Satan has not separated him from the love of God. The Man from Uz knew that he entered the world with nothing and that he would exit the same way. His prosperity, power, prestige, and progeny were only a loan drawn from the bank of heaven. He praised God for the time he got to enjoy his kids. He expressed gratitude for his season of success, the luxuries that flowed from it, and the good times they afforded him. But he never forgot that they were God's to give and take away. Rather than becoming angry or bitter, he praised God for the years he got to enjoy them. In this graveyard praise song, Job sets the gold standard for maturity.

SO FAR, SO GOOD

Job 1:22 puts the exclamation mark on how well the man from Uz passed his first test: "In all this Job did not sin by charging God with wrongdoing." While lesser people might have lost their heads, this devastated man still feared God and shunned evil. Job proved the words of American writer John D. McDonald: "Integrity doesn't blow in the wind or change with the weather." His prayer proves that he believed that God was all powerful in exercising a Creator King's right to do what he wished with his creation and creatures. But the fact that Job didn't charge God with wrongdoing also shows that he believed that God was all good at the same time.

We may breathe a sigh of relief, but let's not relax in our seats quite yet. The plot is about to thicken. This high stakes drama is just starting to heat up in The Theater of Angels.

STORIES
SET IN STONE

A STUDY GUIDE

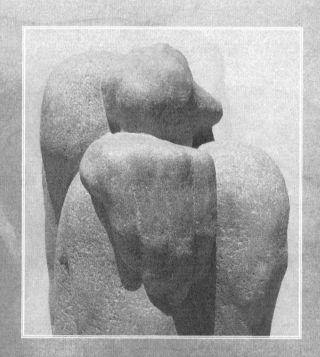

In our last look at Job's story in stone, we saw the oversized left hand of God's compassion over the man's head. We saw Job's weak left arm buried inside his legs. In it we saw the partnership of the ash heap: Job's weak arm of faith and God's strong hand of grace. This time we see how Claudia has used the right hand.

To the artist, this is the hand of strength. Notice how much higher the right shoulder is lifted, and how much less the stronger right arm is burrowed into the body. A huge right hand holds on to Job's right knee. He will not be moved from commitment to God. The Lord's mighty hand will not be moved either. The integrity of God's grace and Job's faith are both too strong to be undone by the mightiest angel's fury.

1. What is the significant difference in the two views of Job's story: "Why do the righteous suffer?" versus "Will the righteous persevere?" Look again at Job 1:11-12. Do you agree that the whole story hangs on this one challenge? How is Satan's challenge the great issue of your salvation and sanctification?

    _____

    _____

    _____

    _____

    _____

    _____

2. The word integrity is at the heart of Job's story. What is your definition of integrity? See how the integrity of our faith is on the line in these verses: Job 1:11, Matthew 7:21-23, Matthew 24:13 and

I John 2:19. See how the integrity of God's grace is put to the test in these verses: Romans 8:30-39 and John 10:27-29.

_____

_____

_____

_____

3. How does Job's prayer at the grave prove the integrity of his faith? See Job 1:20-22. What insights do you get about integrity from his prayer? Look at these verses for further insight: 2 Samuel 12:19-23 and Psalm 30:5

_____

_____

_____

_____

4. How can God still love Job while he is allowing him to go through unspeakable sorrow? See Hebrews 12:6-11. Do we really love our children when we enable them, shield them, or bail them out? Is it possible to allow them to suffer while we weep for their pain, and still keep our hands off knowing that greater good will ultimately come from discipline? How are earthly parents different than our heavenly Father in the matter of discipline?

_____

_____

5. Why doesn't Job blame God? Does it have anything to do with the content of his praise at the grave? Again, see Job 1:20-22. What does he understand that we often miss?

6. Do you agree with John McDonald's statement: "Integrity doesn't blow in the wind and change with the weather."? What does that mean to you?

7. At the grave of Job's children, there is both grief and praise. How can there be both at the same place?

See Philippians 3:10&11. What does "the fellowship of Christ's sufferings" mean, and how does it help us know him better?

See Philippians 4:4-8. What is "the peace that passes all understanding"? How does Paul show us how to get it?

See Hebrews 12:2. What was "the joy set before him" that helped Christ put aside the shame to gain the prize?

" The truly sca
about undisc
is that they h
capacity to d
than the expo

y thing
vered lies
ve a greater
ninish us
sed ones. "

Cheryl Hughes

Act Two: Scene Two

EXPOSED!

THE MOST DELICIOUS MOMENT IN any story is when the clues fall into place, the crime is solved, the perpetrator is unmasked, and the fraud is finally exposed. God specializes in exposing that which is hidden, both the good and the bad. He loves unmasking the deceiver. Jesus saved his angriest rebukes for hypocrites. The word hypocrite comes from the ancient Greek theater. Actors were known as the *hypokrites* or those who wore masks. On the ancient stage, actors morphed from one role to another by simply changing masks.

In a sense, we all wear masks, pretending to be someone we aren't, acting out various roles to earn the approval or applause of others. The rock group *Earth, Wind, and Fire* summed up our fetish with masks in the edgy words of a hit song:

> "Are you really what you see on the inside?
> And hiding what you really are on the inside?
> Pretending that you're something that you're really

not? Everybody wears a face. The whole world is a
masquerade."

Yet God wants us to be transparent. He knows that the
greatest danger in deceiving others is that we end up deceiving
ourselves by believing the lies we tell. After Adam and Eve ate
the forbidden fruit, their eyes were opened and they realized that
they were naked. The first consequence of sin was the introduction of insecurity into the human race. Adam and Eve didn't like
what they saw in themselves. The second result of sin was their
fear that God and others wouldn't accept them as they were. So
they covered themselves with fig leaf aprons.

We still wear our fig leaves. Politicians cover up their pec-
cadillos with excuses. Religious folk hide behind platitudes
and plastic smiles. Scared people fake bravado. Weaklings play
the bully. Closets full of masquerades, cover-ups and lies are
available to us if we feel the need to hide the naked truth about
ourselves. The road to hell is paved with the little deceits that we
employ to maintain the charade.

This is profoundly significant when we look at Job. Satan
has accused him of using his righteousness as a cover-up
for self-serving religion. The Accuser contends that God's
grace is a lot of hocus-pocus that won't sustain Job in the day
of disaster.

Of course, there is great irony in Satan's accusations. Even
as he claims to expose the phoniness of Job's faith and the
fraudulence of God's grace, he is exposing his own hypocrisies.
As the old saying goes, "It takes one to know one." The very flaw
that he wants to expose in Job is his own. Even when he was
heaven's praise leader, his worship was self-serving. When he

didn't get what he wanted, he cursed God to his face. No one is a bigger hypocrite than Lucifer. He is the father of all hypocrites and their hypocrisies.

The lion of hell thinks that he can dismantle and destroy Job's faith. God uses the devil's deceit to prove, and even improve, Job's faith. There is goodness in affliction. Trials and tribulations test the mettle of faith. No one can ever know the strength of steel without testing it with stress. Pity the passengers on the *Titanic* who set out on that ill-fated maiden voyage on an ocean liner with an inadequately tested hull.

We detect the impurities in precious metals by putting them in the refiner's fire. Roots are made stronger or exposed as rotten in the fury of successive storms. We discover our own strengths and weaknesses when we push ourselves to the limits. No pastor will ever know if he is truly a shepherd until the wolf comes. No politician will know if she has integrity until she is called to take a stand that could cost an election.

Afflictions test our faith and expose our flaws. They also prove the reality of our salvation, and are a measuring stick of our sanctification. Non-believers take a closer look at our faith when they see it triumph over adversity. Suffering also gives us greater empathy so that we can comfort others who are going through the same tribulations. The furnace, file, and hammer are brutal, but very useful tools in crafting saints.

CERTAIN TRUTHS IN UNCERTAIN TIMES

Again the emissaries of hell are summoned to the throne of the Most High. The second chapter of Job begins with the same lines as the first. God asks Satan where he's come from. The devil regurgitates the same answer. The Lord asks him again if he's considered Job. This is a strange question in the light of Satan's recent rampage in Uz. God goes on to give the same speech about Job's righteousness. It is so repetitive and redundant, hardly the stuff of good storytelling.

Perhaps what seems to be stale repetition is a literary device to say that, in spite of the fallen angel's best efforts to wreck Job's life, nothing has changed. God is still on the throne. Job is still righteous. Saving grace is still triumphant. Satan is still a liar and a loser. No matter what seems to be falling apart in our world, the truths of Scripture still stand as true in the bad times as in the good. Circumstances cannot change eternal realities.

INTEGRITY IN BOLDFACE

But this second repartee between God and Satan is not as repetitious as it looks on the surface. God adds a new wrinkle in his verbal fencing with this old adversary: "He still maintains his integrity, though you incited me against him to ruin him without any reason." (Job 2:3)

God uses the word *integrity*. As far as we can determine, this is the first time in human history that this word is put down on paper. It is appropriate that God should be the one to introduce it to the world. The Hebrew word describes a seamless piece of cloth with no rips, cuts, or sewn-on fragments. Integrity means that one's life is a single and seamless whole. It is not divided into separate parts.

Job is not a double-minded person. He is righteous when God gives, and just as righteous when God takes away. He doesn't have one faith for the good times and another for the bad. King David spoke the language of integrity when he prayed, "Give me an undivided heart." (Psalm 86:11) Humorist Will Rogers put this spin on integrity: "Live in such a way that you will never be afraid to sell your parrot to the town gossip."

But Satan is convinced that the limits of Job's integrity have not been tested. He is sure that more adversity will crack his righteous resolve. So he lays a hellacious test before God:

> "Skin for skin! A man will give all that he has for
> his life. But stretch out your hand and strike his
> flesh and bones, and he will surely curse you to
> your face."
>
> *—Job 2:4*

The Accuser is saying that a person may be able to handle the loss of prosperity, prestige, and power and still find a way to start over again. This individual may even lose loved ones and still manage to plow through grief. But when it gets down to brass tacks, people love themselves more than anything or anyone else.

"Skin for skin" is an ancient Middle Eastern proverb that asserts the cynical opinion that people will do anything to save their own skin. They will give up family, sell out friends, betray country, and even recant faith. The acid test of folks' integrity is to dismantle their health, ravage their bodies, strip them of their dignity, and force them to endure pain over a prolonged period of time. Surely the cumulative effect of physical pain and degradation will break the sufferer's spirit and destroy what little faith remains.

Again God refuses to strike Job. Instead, he gives Satan permission to ravage his body. This is not unlimited power. This destroyer cannot kill Job. In the agonizing days to come the Man from Uz will surely wish that God had given Satan permission to end his life. He will cry out, "Why did I not perish at birth, and die as I came from the womb?" (Job 3:11) Later he will complain out of his agony, "Why does death not come to those who long for it?" (Job 3:21) What Satan does next beggars the imagination.

Black Leprosy

The lord of darkness wastes no time in flying through unseen airways to the Land of Uz. Job 2:7 says, "He struck Job with painful sores from the soles of his feet to the crown of his head." There isn't a square inch of the man's body that isn't covered with sores. He can't sit down, lie down, get up on his feet, or even stand on his head to get relief.

The King James Version of the Bible says that Job was covered with boils. What exactly was his disease? Most scholars believe that he was afflicted with elephantiasis or black leprosy. Originating in Africa, this dreaded disease is highly contagious and cruelly painful. Of all the diseases on planet earth, this may be the most horrific.

Black leprosy is marked by burning eruptions in the skin that are first red, and then turn black. It envelopes every inch of the victim's skin until the whole body is one burning ulceration. The Hebrew word is not the plural *boils*, but the singular *sore*. Job literally suffers from a whole body sore.

Eventually black leprosy causes the skin to grow crusty and irregular, resembling the skin of an elephant (hence the name elephantiasis). In his complaints over the painful months that follow, Job gives an almost clinical description of black leprosy: intense and unrelenting itching (Job 2;7&8); worms in his open ulcers (Job 7:5); the disintegration of his bones (Job 30:17); the blackening and falling off of his skin (Job 30:30); and terrifying nightmares (Job 7:14).

This disease systematically breaks down the nervous system and addles the mind. The sufferer is usually quarantined because the stench is so unbearable and his appearance utterly grotesque. Mostly, no one else wants to catch this horrifying disease. The worst thing about black leprosy is that it is untreatable and incurable. A death sentence would be preferable to this malady because the poor soul afflicted by it can survive for years. Satan could not have chosen a more devastating and disgusting disease to visit upon the man from Uz. The very fact that the devil chose such a diabolical affliction reminds us of a line about him from Martin Luther's hymn *A Mighty Fortress is our God*:

"For still our ancient foe
  doth seek to work us woe;
  his craft and power are great,
  and armed with cruel hate,
  on earth is not his equal."

The Ash Heap

Job has only a few options, and they are unpalatable. The words of the script are sparse: "Then Job took a piece of broken pottery and scraped himself with it as he sat among the ashes." (Job 2:8) But the imagination paints a vivid scene. Job scoops up mounds of ashes left over from the devastating inferno that has raged across his land. The ashes serve two purposes: they are the only thing soft enough on which to lay an ulcerated body covered with oozing sores; he can also rub these ashes into his skin to give some temporary relief from the unending itching that drives him crazy day and night.

He gyrates constantly from that itching. When the ashes cease to do the work, he finds broken pieces of pottery among the ruins scattered across his property. He uses these chards to scrape at the deeper itch that won't go away. They are also useful for digging out worms that are multiplying in his festering sores.

Once he was manicured and perfumed, hobnobbing with society's elite. People fought to get a seat next to him at a dinner party. Now he is a social pariah. No one wants to get within smelling distance of him. He sits on his ash heap like a shriveled black elephant, covered with blood, scabs, worms, and soot. We recoil in horror and disgust at what we see on center stage at The Theater of Angels. This is no *PG* rated show for the faint of heart. But we must existentially see, smell, and feel the graphic nature of this scene or we will cheat ourselves out of the full impact of what is yet to come.

JOB'S WIFE

For the first time Job's wife appears on stage. She delivers a single angry line, and then stands there tight-lipped while her husband responds with a stinging rebuke. After that, she disappears. Her one line is breathtakingly brutal:

> "Are you still maintaining your integrity? Curse God and die!"
>
> *—Job 2:9*

For that single outburst, this nameless woman has been chastised whenever Job's story is retold. At first blush, our sensibilities are offended by her harshness in the light of her husband's agony. It seems that Satan was clever to leave her untouched so that she could add to her man's torment.

Yet maybe we have treated Mrs. Job unfairly. After all, she gave birth to those ten children who lie in yonder grave. She carried each of them for nine months in her womb, and then nurtured and raised them. No father can ever feel the love that a mother feels for her babies. Her grief must be as painful as his boils. She too lost everything when the disasters struck. She has also been socially ostracized by fair-weather friends.

But the worst thing for Job's wife is watching him suffer. Some of us know what its like to sit by the hospital or hospice bed of a suffering loved one. We watch our sweetheart twitch and moan in pain. We are forced to witness their loss of dignity until we can't bear it anymore. It's easy to become angry at the circumstances or the God who doesn't intervene. We secretly hope that our beloved will quietly slip away into eternity. When our dear one passes away we are filled with a mixture of grief and relief.

Job's wife can't bear to watch another day of her husband's suffering. Her heartache has turned to bitterness and anger. She knows that Job's stubborn refusal to give up on God is somehow behind his unrelenting torment. If her husband would just curse God, the Most High might strike him dead and put an end to his misery. She also recognizes the awesome power of faith that keeps her man going when lesser men would have given up. She concludes that, if only he would abandon that faith, a merciful end would come so much sooner.

While you are weeping for Job, shed some tears for the dear wife whose unspeakable heartache has shattered her soul, ravaged her faith, and turned her shrill with bitter rage.

INTEGRITY'S REBUKE

Job shuts his wife off with a stinging rebuke: "You are speaking like a foolish woman! Shall we accept good from God, but not trouble?" (Job 2:10) It's no wonder that his wife exits so quickly. We are as shocked by his harshness toward his wife as we were by her brutal assault on him. We should not be surprised. The cumulative effect of pain has worn Job's emotions as raw as his ulcerated skin. He is on the ragged edge emotionally. But then, so is Mrs. Job. When husband and wife are equally wounded by devastation, the house can become a war zone. Dutch priest and psychologist Henri Nouwen often warned, "Hurting people hurt people."

Relationships are often the first casualties of suffering. That's why it's important to be patient with hurting people. If you are the care-giver, don't take personally the harsh things that your suffering loved ones might say when patience is worn down to a nub. If you are the one in pain, be aware of the wear and tear that your care-giver is experiencing in ministering to you day after day. When the season of suffering is over, let go of the insensitive and hurtful things that were said in the pressure cooker of dealing with that which overwhelms. Satan delights in the dogfight between Job and his wife. This too is part of his strategy to dismantle and destroy Job's faith. We can expect the same thing in our sufferings.

Yet, in spite of his harshness, Job's response to his wife's demand that he abandon his integrity is the perfect definition of the word *integrity*:

> "Shall we accept good from God, but not bad?"
>
> —Job 2:10

He has lost everything but his bitter wife. Yet, whether times are good or bad, his faith remains the same. He will be just as content with nothing as he was with everything. He will worship God on the ash heap as surely as he praised him in his mansion. Job is telling us that integrity is the inner core of one's being that doesn't blow in the wind or change with the weather. One's belief system must be lived out in suffering with the same integrity that it is in success.

U.S. Senator Alan Simpson's political career was in jeopardy because his core values required him to take an unpopular stand on an explosive issue. When someone asked him why he was willing to sacrifice so much for a principle, he responded, "If you have integrity, nothing else matters. If you don't have integrity, nothing else matters."

In an age when politicians sell their souls to win elections, CEOs prostitute their values to make a profit, pastors redefine biblical truth to fill their churches, and parishioners abandon God when life throws them a curve ball, Job is refreshingly rare. It's no wonder God said, "There is no one on earth like him."

Integrity defined the way Job handled success in life. When riches and respect were being lavished on him, he remained blameless and upright. Abraham Lincoln wrote, "Nearly all men can stand adversity, but if you want to test a man's character, give him power." Conversely, when he lost it all, he was still blameless and upright. As Samuel Richardson put it, "Calamity is the test of integrity."

Affluence and affliction will equally test integrity. Yet the issue of integrity is bigger than Job. God's integrity is also on the line in the land of Uz. Does God's truth stand the test of the good times and the bad? Is God's grace as amazing in the storms as it is in the sunshine? Can anything separate us from his love, or any tribulation keep a redeemed child of God from his or her ultimate triumph?

Job is being systematically dismantled by the devil's cruelty. Yet this fallen angel's accusations against God and Job are also being dismantled in the process. Job 2:10 ends with the words, "In all this, Job did not sin in what he said." The more Job is stripped naked, the more his integrity is exposed. People of integrity don't need masks or fig leaves.

In a delicious twist of irony, Satan's accusations are also exposed as lies. This too is one of the great benefits of our afflictions. They expose the weaknesses in our character that need to be fixed as well as the strengths that we never knew we possessed. Our season on the ash heap also exposes the devil as a liar and the promises of God's Word to be true.

INTEGRITY'S TEST NEVER ENDS

Now the lights dim on center stage. A scene change is in the offing. Maybe this is a good time for you and me to take a deep breath and reflect on what we have just witnessed. Remember one person's story is everyone's story, including yours and mine. Have you settled the issue of integrity in your own life? Can you make Job's confession your own?

> I will accept the bad things from God as surely as
> I accept the good things that he sends my way.

It's easy to mouth Job's faith affirmation when sitting in The Theater of Angels watching his agony on the ash heap. It will require God's grace and all the fortitude you can muster up when you are sitting on your own heap of ashes. Like all the other questions Job's story has forced us to answer, this one is best settled before the tough times come.

Let's return to the drama on stage. Job still sits alone in agony on ashes. The worst is yet to come. If he survives the onslaught that is waiting in the wings, he will have withstood his greatest test in The Theater of Angels.

STORIES
SET IN STONE

A STUDY GUIDE

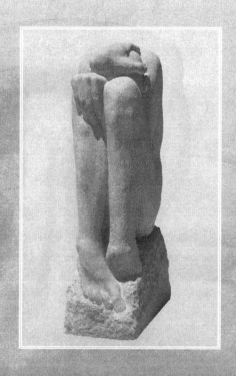

The softness of the ashes may bring relief to a boil. But they are also all that remains of everything Job once held precious. It can't be easy to feel, smell, and rub into your body the evidence of destruction. It is here that Job viscerally feels his personal shame, the loss of his wife's support and his standing in the community.

Satan banked on the fact that, when it comes to their own skin, people will betray morals, family, country, and God. He is wrong about Job! Claudia shows Job's tenacity in his feet. Though they are twisted in agony, toes dig deep into the ash heap. One foot is all the way in at a grotesque angle of pain. He will not allow the ashes of destruction to move him from God's appointed place.

Jesus set his face toward the cross, and walked steadfastly to the ash heap God had appointed for him. His feet were nailed to that diabolical instrument of death. He did not save his skin at the expense of our souls. Let this guide your reflections and discussions as you come to grips with integrity.

1. Adam and Eve put on fig leaves (see Genesis 3:7-11). Why? What are the fig leaves we wear, and why? What did Jesus say about mask wearing? See Matthew 6:1-24 & 24:12-39.

---

2. How does affliction rip off our mask? How does a proper response to our suffering rip off Satan's mask? How do afflictions prove our salvation? See Matthew 5:12, James 1:16, 2 John 2:19. How are they the measure of our sanctification? See Romans 5:3, Hebrews 11:1&2, James 1:2-4, James 5:11.

_____

_____

_____

_____

_____

_____

_____

3. Do you agree with the author that the repetition in Job 1:6-8 and Job 2:1-3 are a literary device to show that, no matter how many tough times we go through, nothing ultimately changes? See Ecclesiastes 1:9. Satan is still deceitful (see John 8:44). God is still on the throne (see Isaiah 40:21-31). Job's faith is still intact. (Job 1:22-21) See also Jeremiah 1:15, Malachi 3:16, and Ephesians 3:9-12.

_____

_____

_____

_____

_____

_____

_____

_____

4. Yet, doesn't one thing change? See 2 Corinthians 3:18.

5. Satan says "skin for skin." Why is our own skin the ultimate test of our integrity? See Genesis 3:2, Job 2:4&5, Mark 14:66-72, Matthew 24:10, 1 Timothy 4:1.

6. What was your reaction to the author's description of black leprosy? Could you handle this without caving in? See 2 Corinthians 10:13, Hebrews 7:25, Luke 22:32. Does God give supernatural grace to handle what is beyond our natural ability?

7. Are we fair to criticize Job's wife? Is Job too harsh in his criticism of his wife in Job 2:10? What did you learn about dealing with suffering folk from their interchange in Job 2:9&10? Job 2:10 says that Job did not sin. Does that mean that he didn't sin against Mrs. Job?

8. Job goes from one test to another. Is there ever an end to the testing of our integrity? Think about Abraham, Moses, David, Peter, and Paul. Did their testing ever end this side of the grave? What do we learn from the fact that, of the 400 leaders in the Bible, only 11 went all the way without a serious stumble, most having their biggest failure after 50 years of age?

EXPOSED

AUTHOR'S NOTE

The amount of Scripture covered in the following chapter, *Job's Comforters*, together with the breadth and depth of discussion questions, make it advisable to divide this up into two small group sessions. This would make the total number of Small Group Bible studies add up to twelve.

" God save me friends, I can myself from

rom my
protect
y enemies. "

Claude Louis Hector De Villars

*Act **Two:*** *Scene Three*

JOB'S
COMFORTERS

AS THIS SCENE OPENS, THE stage is ominously dark. The awful
silence portends that something sinister is about to take place.
A single circle of light slowly envelops the solitary man sitting
on his pile of ashes. Aside from him, the set is starkly empty.
Deprived of any other sensory perception, we are forced to look
again at the grotesqueness of this black leper who oozes blood
mingled with pus and soot. The stench is more than we can bear.
We want to hold our noses and avert our eyes, but that which
repulses also fascinates.

The real pathos is in the utter loneliness of the afflicted man.
His creature comforts are gone. His children have been taken
away. His wife has deserted him. His servants are in hiding, pretending not to hear his cries for help. His relatives are nowhere
to be found. Country club friends want nothing to do with him.
One can almost hear the plaintive lyrics and achingly sad melody

of Roy Orbison's golden classic softly playing in the background: "Only the lonely know the way I feel tonight."

Job desperately needs some comfort. We all do when life leaves us teetering on the ragged edge. When Jeremiah was stumbling through the wreckage of Jerusalem after the Babylonian holocaust, he lamented,

> "There is no one here to comfort me, no one
> to restore my spirit."
>
> —*Lamentations 1:16*

This is the brokenness that is worse than ulcers that itch and ooze. A person's spirit can endure sickness and loss. Job has proven that. But what can sustain us when the spirit is finally broken? When our days are bleakest, we are most in need of friends. God commands us, "Comfort, comfort my people." (Isaiah 40:1) St. Paul instructs Christians, "Comfort one another." (I Thessalonians 4:18) Loneliness cannot be sustained indefinitely. God not only created us for himself, he has made us for one another. Worship and community are the twin sisters of our deepest need, especially in times of great pain.

JOB'S FRIENDS

Off stage we hear shuffling feet and voices. Comfort has finally arrived with Job's three best friends, Eliphaz the Temanite, Bildad the Shuhite, and Zophar the Naamathite. (Job 2:11) A fourth man lags behind. He's not mentioned now, but he will be identified later as "Elihu, the son of Barachel the Buzite of the family of Ram." (Job 32:2) This young man was probably invited to accompany one of Job's three friends. As is the custom of the Middle East, he will sit quietly in deference to his elders.

This is no small show of friendship. Eliphaz journeyed several hundred miles across rugged wilderness from Teman in the mountains of what is now Jordan, most likely accompanied by Elihu who came from the same region. Bildad trekked out of the burning deserts of Arabia. Zophar tramped almost a thousand miles from Canaan. These men have traveled weeks and months, at great danger and cost, to comfort their friend.

If we do a rough calculation of how long it took for the news of Job's disasters to get to them, and then how much time elapsed as they arranged their trip and traveled to Uz, it is no stretch to say that Job had already spent the worst part of the year suffering from black leprosy. How many prayers for healing have gone up from his ash heap in those long months? Yet God has remained silent. By the time his friends arrive, Job is ravaged beyond recognition. They are horrified.

> "When they saw him from a distance, they could hardly recognize him; they began to weep aloud, and tore their robes and sprinkled dust on their heads. Then they sat on the ground with him for seven days and seven nights. No one said a word to him, because they saw how great his suffering was."
> —Job 2:11-13

GOOD COMFORT

After months of uninterrupted suffering, Job has seven days of comforting from his friends. Psalm 133:1&2 says,

"How good and pleasant is it when brothers live
together in unity! It is like precious oil poured on
the head, running down on the beard..."

When we are suffering affliction, friends who come to offer
their comfort are like soothing oil poured out on the dryness
of a brittle soul. The best comfort comes from those who can
empathize with our struggles because they've been there themselves. Most of us have had that visit from the sweet Christian
who tries to soften our pain with pious platitudes. Even biblical
truths can ring hollow when we are on the ash heap of suffering
while the one spouting them is in good health. Joe Baily lost
three children. After one of his kids died, he wrote *A View from
the Hearse*. In it he recalls his comforters with mixed reviews:

"I was sitting, torn by grief. Someone came and
talked to me of God's dealings, of why it happened,
and of hope beyond the grave. He talked constantly.
He said things I knew were true. I was unmoved,
except to wish he would go away. He finally did.

Another came and sat beside me. He didn't talk.
He didn't ask me leading questions . He just sat
beside me for an hour or more, listened when I said
something, answered briefly, prayed simply, and
then left. I was moved. I was comforted. I hated
to see him go."

There are no handbooks with easy formulas for showing mercy
that will satisfy every sufferer at all times. Comfort requires great

sensitivity in each situation. It should be bathed in prayer for Holy Spirit direction. Yet, when a friend is on the ash heap of suffering, we can at least do the five things that Job's comforters did at first.

❶ Be There

It took a herculean effort for those four to make their long and dangerous journeys to Job's bedside in the Land of Uz. Nothing says "I care" more than making the time to come. We are often afraid to show up because we don't know what to say. What we blurt out might make things worse. We don't want to be disturbed by the sights and smells of suffering. We dread looking at a reality that we might experience someday. It was risky business for Job's friends to come as comforters, and it will be risky for us. But, we should be there anyway!

❷ Be Real

We don't have to fake our feelings. Job's comforters didn't try to make him feel better with church lady plastic smiles or rosy platitudes. That would have been dishonest to their Middle Eastern culture. They responded by lifting their voices in loud wailing, ripping their robes, and pouring dirt on their heads. (Job 2:12) A visceral show of empathy is soothing to the sufferer. If we feel like shedding tears, we should do it. If we don't have anything to say, it's okay to be quiet. If we don't have answers, we can honestly admit it. Few sufferers expect comforters to be perfect, but vulnerability and transparency are almost always appreciated.

❸ Be Quiet

After their initial outburst of grief, Job's comforters sat down next to the ash heap for seven days and nights without opening

THE THEATER OF ANGELS

their mouths. This should fill us with amazement. We live in an age when lulls in conversation are embarrassingly uncomfortable. We too often babble on in the presence of the silent sufferer. We forget Solomon's sage advice: "...many words mark the speech of a fool..." (Ecclesiastes 5:3) But Job's friends sat silently by their suffering friend for 168 straight hours. They didn't open their mouths until Job spoke first. The grotesque disfiguration of Job must have been appalling and his stench nauseating, but they continued to sit there silently out of respect for his suffering.

If we take these seven days figuratively, as some scholars do, there is another powerful lesson: Seven is the Hebrew number for perfection. There is a perfect time to speak. God will reveal it to us, and give us the right words to say. For this reason alone, we should never fear going to the ash heap of a suffering friend.

4 Be Supportive

The point of going to the ash heap of a sufferer isn't to make yourself feel better by playing the Good Samaritan for a few minutes. Nor are we there to defend God, correct bad theology, or rebuke cynical words born out of a sufferer's pain. The ash heap may develop stronger faith, but it also births raw emotions, hopeless despair, and even doubt and unbelief. We may be shocked by the heretical outbursts of those on the ragged edge, but we aren't there to fix their attitudes or defend God's reputation. The Most High is quite capable of doing both. We are simply there to support the afflicted the best we can.

When it comes to being supportive to those on the ash heap, it is important to remember Job's wife. There is no indication that Job's friends looked in on her. We are often so focused on those who are afflicted that we forget the emotional pain of their loved ones. When my dear wife went through a serious bout with cancer, people would often pass right by Rachael and me to give Joyce words of comfort. But our little girl and I were silently grieving at the possibility of spending the rest of our lives without the woman we loved most in the world. Though we were glad to see people rally around Joyce, we were grateful to those who paused to minister to our hurts too.

5 Be Available

Certainly, Job's friends were available. Lots of folks will visit the hospital, surround the family during the time of crisis, and be there at the funeral when sickness or accident ends in death. Most of us are attracted to times of high drama. But there are precious few who will be there to offer ongoing care during the long months of recuperation. Not many will remember to look in on the grieving person during the holidays or other special days when their loss is most painful. As time goes on, comforters forget and drop by the wayside. Few people are aware that grief and loneliness require long term nurture.

CRUEL COMFORT

Not only did Job's comforters sit silently by the ash heap for 168 straight hours, so did the man sitting on it. Sometimes pain reduces us to muteness. We've said everything there is to say, but it hasn't brought us solace. We've heard everything that others have said, but it hasn't given us peace. We've prayed for hours on end, but it hasn't provided us healing or tranquility. We have exhausted our thinking, but answers remain shrouded in mystery. It hurts too much to open our mind, ears, or mouth any more. In a rare interview, Rose Kennedy talked about why she had so little to say about the well-known tragedies of her life, including the untimely deaths of a daughter, Kathleen, and three sons, Joseph, Jack, and Bobby:

> "It has been said that time heals all wounds. I do not agree. The wounds remain. In time, the mind, protecting its sanity, covers them with scar tissue and the pain lessons, but it's never gone."

In his classic book *The Problem of Pain,* C.S. Lewis spoke of how much easier it is to talk about physical pain than mental anguish. Lewis says that we are more apt to hide mental distress because we don't want to be labeled as unstable. But the frequent attempts to conceal mental pain only increases the weight of the burden. It is much easier to tell others that our tooth is aching than it is to say, "My heart is breaking."

The Risks of Transparency

Empathy is like oil that loosens the rusty hinges on doors of silence. The sustained compassion of his friends encourages Job to open up. Yet his bottled-up emotions have been festering inside for so long that his words wash over his stunned friends like a torrent of raw sewage.

In all the years they've known this righteous man, Job's comforters have never heard this kind of language come out of his mouth. They see nothing blameless or upright in the bitter anger that he spews out. Nor do they see any fear of God in his words. Perhaps the afflicted keep silent precisely because they know that the dark feelings pent up inside would shock and scandalize people (if they were ever rash enough to let it all hang out).

Job's friends are righteously indignant, and unable to contain their outrage. For the better part of the remaining script of this drama, they get into a heated theological debate with the man on the ash heap; point and counterpoint, accusation and refutation, blame and excuse, tit for tat, back and forth.

We must be as fair to Job's comforters as we were to his embittered wife. Job's outburst shows that he is out on the ledge, seemingly ready to jump off. His friends start out trying to talk him back in off that ledge. Job takes some harsh jabs at God. His friends feel duty-bound to defend their Creator and Lord. Job says that he has done nothing wrong to deserve all the bad that's happened to him. His buddies reason that he must be lacking in something, or God wouldn't have allowed him to suffer in such horrible ways.

At the Crux of the Matter

The debate will now go on for twenty-eight chapters of Job's story, lasting the better part of a single long day. Few readers stay engaged at this point. Most folks are easily caught up in the drama in the first two chapters, and then skip to the end where Job gets double blessing and lives happily ever after. They quickly lose patience with the theological debates in between. Yet the angels in the theater now sit forward on the edges of their seats. They know that this dialogue is at the crux of the whole matter.

When we skip through these pages of script, we are cheating ourselves out of this story's richest moments. This is at the very heart of Job's drama. Those who have suffered deeply have most likely thought or said everything that Job utters from his ash heap. Everyone who has ever wrestled with the *why* questions has speculated the same things that are expressed in this dialogue between friends. These chapters contain the final assault on Job's soul. It is here that Job's supreme battle will be fought and his ash heap afflictions redeemed. Here you will experience the crescendo and climax. So put on your seat belts and get ready for a roller coaster ride of highs and lows, ending with heaven's great intervention and triumph.

Job's Complaint

This is the resounding snap. The final straw breaks. Job curses the day of his birth. (Job 3:1) A tsunami of self-pity gushes forth. But no complaint is bigger than this one: "Why did I not perish at birth, and die as I came from the womb?" (Job 3:11) Every one of us who has endured what St. John of the Cross called "the dark night of the soul" has had a moment of raw honesty when we wished that we had never been born. We've probably voiced Job's other complaint too: why can't I just die and escape my misery once and for all? (Job 3:20-22)

This is a moment of high drama. For the first time Job crosses the line by charging God with wrongdoing. His accusation mirrors the bitterness of his wife: why does God give life only to allow it to be turned into hell on earth? Why does he keep the afflicted alive when they desperately want to die? Job's anger has caused his pious platitudes to turn into honest-to-God transparency. All the masks are ripped off.

His perspective has been flipped upside down. In pleasant days, he believed that God had put a hedge of protection around his prosperous life. Now God's hedge imprisons him on the ash heap and keeps him from escaping to the grave. The God of grace has become his jailer. Job's cynicism matches what Martin Luther wrote about his own season of despair: "I lost touch with Christ the Savior and Comforter, and made him the jailor and hangman of my poor soul."

The rebuke that he earlier gave his wife has been forgotten. The seamless cloth of his integrity is beginning to unravel. The lion of hell has his teeth locked around Job's juggler, and his faith is slowly asphyxiating. Is it possible that the Man from Uz is dangerously close to cursing God? Surely, the fallen angels and demons of hell are now anticipating a celebration of victory in The Theater of Angels.

Godly Comfort turns to Godless Debate

Eliphaz is scandalized by Job's audacity to charge God with wrongdoing. He rebukes the man on the ash heap with the cruelest of jabs: You used to talk a good game when you counseled those who were suffering. Yet, when you are down on your luck, you don't practice what you preach. (Job 4:3-4)

In the original text of Job 4:6, the word integrity is used for the third time in this story. Only now, Eliphaz accuses Job of having lost his. The comforter from Teman pontificates about the brutality of fallen creation where old lions starve to death and man is born for trouble. He argues that suffering is visited on earth by a righteous God who disciplines the wayward and punishes the wicked. (Job 4&5) He tells Job that the innocent have never perished, implying that maybe his friend isn't so innocent after all. (Job 4:6&7) He tells Job to rejoice because God is disciplining him for some unrecognized sin. He piously concludes, "Happy is the man whom God corrects. Therefore, do not despise the chastening of the Almighty." (Job 5:17 *KJV*)

Job has heard enough. Is there anything worse than being kicked while down? He rebukes Eliphaz by arguing that a true friend would treat his afflicted buddy with kindness, even if he abandoned God altogether. (Job 5:14)

Job challenges all of us at this point. Will we allow our friends to open up and be honest, even if it makes us feel uncomfortable? Will we stick with our brothers and sisters in the Faith, even if they have doubts about God? When folks are on the ash heap of affliction, or suffering post traumatic stress afterwards, they may need our comfort more than correction.

Job confronts Eliphaz, "How painful are your honest words! But what do your arguments prove?" (Job 6:25) Correct theology that brings no comfort is useless and cruel. What good is it to win the debate and lose the person? Job continues to bang this point home as he continues his rant all the way through the seventh chapter.

Bildad Jumps In

This dialogue at the ash heap begins to look like a tag team match in a World Federation Wrestling extravaganza. Eliphaz has finished thrashing Job (for the moment). Now Bildad jumps into the ring to continue the pummeling. Whereas Eliphaz was the orthodox defender of the Faith, Bildad is the proponent of the Prosperity Gospel. He argues that God always rewards the righteous. If we are suffering sickness or poverty it is because we are harboring some hidden sin or lack of faith. He counsels Job that, if he searches his heart to discover what he has done wrong and returns fully to God, he can count on renewed blessings. He assures Job that the seed faith formula always works: "He will yet fill your mouth with laughter and your lips with joy." (Job 8:21)

Job meekly agrees with Bildad: "Indeed, I know that this is true." (Job 9:2) Then he reverses course and lays out an argument that devastates the premise of Bildad's prosperity gospel: no one can ever exercise enough faith to earn God's blessings. His glory is so great that we all fall short of it. If we had to depend on the seed of our goodness for a harvest of blessings, we would all be doomed.

Suddenly, Job's logic is skewed on the horns of a dilemma: if no one is good enough to please God, neither is he. By his own words, he has condemned himself to the horrors of the ash heap. He cries out to God,

> "Even if I wash myself with soap and my hands with
> cleansing powder, you would plunge me into a
> slime pit so that even my clothes would detest me."
> —*Job 9:30&31*

But soon after grasping how far short of God's glory that he has fallen, Job again reverts to a defense of his own goodness. He complains that he doesn't deserve the bad things that have happened to him. Rabbi Kushner would applaud what Job says next about God in the presence of Bildad and his buddies:

> "...I will give free reign to my complaint and speak
> out of the bitterness of my soul...does it please you
> to oppress me, to spurn the works of your hands,
> while you smile on the plans of the wicked?"
> —*Job 10:1&3*

All of us who have suffered a prolonged and deeply painful season on our own ash heap know about the wild mood swings born out of affliction. One minute faith soars on wounded wings. Then, it crashes on jagged rocks of bitter doubt and despair. Faith on the ash heap is often schizophrenic. This is more than an emotional roller coaster ride for Job. The outcome of the battle is in doubt. Job is dangerously close to cursing God. Does the devil's wager seem ready to pay off? Or will Faith triumph?

Zophar Gets in a Few Licks

The man from the coast of Canaan jumps into the fray. There's nothing that religious types love more than to pile on the heretic. It's now three against one. Zophar is the nastiest one of all: the purveyor of the *ad hominem* argument (that's Latin for argument "against the man"). For the frustrated debater, this is the argument of last resort. If you can't win on the merits of your logic, then assassinate your opponent's character. Resort to name calling. Diminish a differing viewpoint by putting a label on the person who holds it: left wing extremist, right wing nut job, bigot, or heretic. The *ad hominem* argument is the last refuge of the scoundrel.

Zophar tries to browbeat Job into submission by ridiculing him as an idle talker or just another empty suit. (Job 11:3) He follows up with a punch to the gut: "For you have said, 'My beliefs are flawless and I am pure in your sight." (Job 11:4) Sarcasm drips from Zophar's words. He continues with one stinging kidney punch after another as he mocks Job's complaints about God's unfair treatment.

Having softened up the doubter, Zophar becomes the impassioned evangelist. He pleads with Job to come to the altar of repentance: "Yet if you devote your heart to him, and stretch out your hand to him, if you put away the sin in your hand..." (Job 11:13&14) When tearful pleading doesn't work, Zophar switches to hell-fire-and-damnation: "But the eyes of the wicked will fail, and escape will elude them; their hope will become a dying gasp." (Job 11:20) Zophar the evangelist is telling Job that if he doesn't turn, he will surely burn.

Job is at the end of his patience. For the better part of a year he has suffered unending ruin and degradation. Now he is being ganged up on by his comforters. There is nothing worse than the pious accusations of the pompous. In chapters 12-14, Job has a meltdown and blasts his buddies for their ignorant assumptions and arrogant accusations.

Having unloaded on his friends, Job takes aim at God. "If you have a problem with me, come out with it!" (Job 13:23) "Quit hiding your face!" (Job 13:24) "Stop tormenting me!" (Job 13:25) Job is calling God out. His rant against the Lord goes all the way through the 14th chapter. Job teaches us that it's okay to be honest with God. He knows our deepest pains and doubts. He has no insecurities. He can handle our complaints and listen to our heresies with far more patience than most religious folk. Hiding our festering doubts behind a plastic smile only makes us more dysfunctional.

The Gospel Peaks through the Clouds

Eliphaz jumps back into the ring for another shot at Job. There is nothing more infuriating to self-appointed Defenders of the Faith than a heretic who won't fall quickly into line. In the fifteenth chapter of Job's story, he again thrashes the black leper for accusing an all powerful God of not being all good:

> "Why has your heart carried you away, and why do your eyes flash, so that you vent your rage against God and pour out such words from your mouth?"
> —Job 15:12&13

Eliphaz is like Apollo Creed in the first *Rocky* movie. He throws everything he has at the punch drunk fighter, and still the bum won't go down for the count. When a battered and bloodied Rocky gets up for the umpteenth time, Creed shouts in frustration, "Why don't you just stay down?" Most of us have had that Eliphaz moment where we just want that suffering person to stop wearing us out with incessant complaints and ungodly attitudes.

Job refuses to stay down on the canvas. He swings back at Eliphaz, "Will your long-winded speeches never end? What ails you that you keep on arguing?" (Job 16:3) Bildad jumps back into the ring for one more go at Job, delivering yet another hell-fire-and-brimstone description of the place where God consigns those who don't shape up and fly right. (Job 18) Bildad's tactics don't intimidate Job. He feels like he has already been to hell and back. He counterpunches with this angry retort:

> "My relatives have gone astray; my closest friends
> have forgotten me. My guests and my female
> servants count me a foreigner; they look on me as
> on a stranger. I summon my servant, but he does
> not answer, though I beg him with my own mouth.
> My breath is offensive to my wife; I am loathsome
> to my own family. Even the little boys scorn me;
> when I appear, they ridicule me; my intimate friends
> detest me; those I love have turned against me.
> I am nothing but skin and bones. I have escaped
> only by the skin of my teeth."
>
> *—Job 19:14-20*

As he recounts the horrors of the past year, and adds to them the bullying of his comforters, the man on the ash heap grabs hold of the only hope left to him:

> "I know that my redeemer lives, and that in the end
> he will stand on the earth."
>
> —Job 19:25

Earlier, as he agonized over his alienation from God, he had cried out, "If only there was someone to mediate between us, someone to bring us together." (Job 9:33) The Hebrew word for mediator speaks of someone who stands between two adversaries, puts a hand on each person's shoulder, and then draws them together. Since Adam and Eve rebelled against their Creator, there has been enmity between sinful humanity and a holy God. Job's comforters believe that prodigal children earn their way back into the Father's house by being good enough. Job knows better. As upright and blameless as he has been, he is still alienated from God.

He desperately wishes for a mediator some 2,000 years before God sent his Only Begotten Son to earth. Though Job may not know exactly who that Mediator will be, he sees a shadow of the One who will hang on a cross outside Jerusalem, his arms outstretched on the crossbeam, a nail-pierced hand reaching for the shoulders of God's lost children, and another for the shoulder of his Father in heaven. At the cross, the Mediator brings lost sinner and holy God together. He is Job's Redeemer, and the Savior of all those who look to his finished work on the cross as the only basis of their salvation.

The man on the ash heap says, "I know that my Redeemer

lives..." (Job 19:25) On the third day Christ rose from his grave. All of Satan's fury at Golgotha couldn't defeat him. Death couldn't hold him. Job declares, "...and I will see him in the land of the living." (Job 19:25) This man from Uz is the first person in the Bible to speak of the resurrection from the dead. If our Redeemer has risen from the dead, so will those of us who have been saved by his work.

The gospel has redeemed Job's afflictions. Though his body is ravaged with disease, he sees through the mists of pain to a hill far away where another mangled body hangs on a Roman cross. He sees the triumph of that Redeemer, and the hope of his own victory.

In yet another moment of illumination, he declared the ultimate meaning of faith: "Though he slay me, yet will I hope in him." (Job 13:15) Suffering not only drives us deep into despair and doubt, it also gives us wings to fly into the rarified air of dazzling spiritual insight and clarity.

Integrity Settles the Issue

After a person has seen the goodness of God's grace in Christ, all else pales in significance. Yet through seven more grueling chapters, Job and his comforters continue to slug it out. Though the gospel gives us the assurance of our ultimate salvation, it does not spare us from an interim season of struggles with our flesh. It is in wrestling with our abiding sins that we are transformed into the likeness of our Redeemer. In fact, that is the whole point of our salvation. St. Paul wrote, "For those God foreknew he also predestined to be conformed to the image of his Son..." (Romans 8:29)

There is a great moment of triumph when Job finally puts

a stop to his comforter's assumptions and accusations. He no longer has to prove himself to others. He will live or die by the judgment of his Father in heaven. Perhaps, for many of us, the moment of victory is when we no longer feel the need to justify ourselves, compare ourselves to others, or work for the applause of people.

If we can come to the point where we live to please God alone, find our salvation in him alone, our satisfaction in him alone, and know that he alone has our best interests at heart, then we will find the integrity that we need to live upright and blameless lives in the worst of circumstances. With quiet defiance, Job shuts up the mouths of his accusers:

> "I will never admit you are in the right; till I die
> I will not deny my integrity. I will maintain my
> innocence and never let go of it; my conscience
> will not reproach me as long as I live."
>
> —Job 27:5&6

There's that word integrity again. It dominates this story. Satan has exhausted his full arsenal on Job. The man's faith has been tested to the outer limits of human endurance. It has been strained to the point of snapping. Job has teetered on the ragged edge of unbelief, ready to jump off into the abyss of abandoned faith. More than once Satan thought he had him down for the count. The fallen angels and demons must have whistled and hooted with devilish delight from their section of The Theater of Angels.

Yet integrity has won the day. Job's faith is triumphant. He will not deny God, even if his Redeemer should decide to slay him.

He knew that, no matter what happens, he will see him again in the land of the living.

God's grace is triumphant too. Nothing can separate a redeemed ash heap man from the love of God in Christ Jesus our Lord. Satan may be crafty, but God is all wise, all powerful, and all good. The Lord High Protector of England in the 1600's, Oliver Cromwell wrote, "Subtlety may deceive you, integrity never will." Satan has lost the day. He always does when he tangles with God. The half-brother of Jesus was right after all:

> "Resist the devil, and he will flee from you. Draw
> near to God and he will draw near to you."
> *--James 4:8&9*

If Job's story is yours, then his victory can surely be yours too. Dear friend, perhaps you are going through the worst of it right now. Even your comforters have brought you little or no comfort. Don't let the words of people deter you from holding on to the truths of Scripture. Job came to the point where victory is always grasped from the jaws of defeat. He was willing to say, "Though he slay me, yet will I hope in him." (Job 13:15) Have you come to that point yet? Only then can you say with St. Paul, "*Nothing* will be able to separate us from the love of God that is in Christ Jesus our Lord." (Romans 8:39)

There's Still More to Come

The hero has won, but don't leave the theater yet. The young man Elihu has some good lines you don't want to miss. God himself will make an entrance on center stage. He has some business to settle with Job and his comforters, and maybe with you and me too. There are plenty of fireworks still left in this drama. So take a break, catch your breath, and come back when the curtain rises on the final act.

STORIES
SET IN STONE
A STUDY GUIDE

Claudia's sculpture of Job captures the tightening of his body at the cruel assault of his comforters. Their initial empathy had made him feel safe enough to vent his honest rage. They saw it as sacrilege that demanded their correction.

Notice that his body is stull hunched in pain and agony. His head is bowed in shame under their withering assault. But the left hand of God's compassionate grace is still there. His head remains, bowed, waiting for God to make sense of it all.

Yet his left ear is open to hearing something from them. The left is the feminine side for artists. Job desperately needs words of compassion. Instead he gets corrective theology. Yet his ear remains open. It's hard to listen when what we hear is unpleasant and not entirely true. If we don't close off our ears to the stupidities of others, we may well miss words from God. Now it's time for you to listen for God, and to each other. These questions are given to spark reflection and discussion.

1.   Is comforting the afflicted an option or command? See Isaiah 40:13-18, Matthew 7:12, Matthew 24:34-41, Romans 12:15, 1 Thessalonians 4:13-18. Why do you think that we find it so hard to comfort others, especially long-term nurturing?

THE THEATER OF ANGELS

2. Were there any "aha" moments for you in the initial good comfort of Job 2:11-13? Reflect on and discuss the five rules of good comfort: be there, be real, be quiet, be supportive, and be available. Which is most important to you? Which do you think is most violated by well-meaning Christians?

    _____

    _____

    _____

    _____

    _____

    _____

3. List the afflicted man's complaints in Job 3. Does anything he says shock you? Are his comforters right to think what he says is theologically incorrect, if not even sacrilegious?

    _____

    _____

    _____

    _____

    _____

4. How should we respond when our empathy causes the afflicted to spew out their darkest thoughts? See Job 5:14 & 6:25, I Kings 19:3-6, Galatians 6:1? Is it our job to defend God, or even ourselves when our sincere efforts are rebuffed?

    _____

    _____

5. Later God rebukes Job's comforters. What did they do wrong? When should we correct bad theology, and when should we keep quiet? When does debate become godless? See Job 4:3-5.

6. Is Eliphaz right when he says that suffering is God's punishment for sin? See Job 15:3-6. How do his assumptions square up with Job 9:2, I Peter 4:12&13, John 19:30, Job 1:8?

7. Eliphaz says that Job should rejoice in his suffering. See Job 16:1-8. If James 1:2-4 says the same thing, why is Job so angry at Eliphaz?

See Job 16:1-8. What are the top three worst pious platitudes that you have heard? Do they make you angry like Job, and why?

_____

_____

_____

_____

_____

8. What do you think of Bildad's Prosperity Gospel? See Job 8. If God without fail blesses us for our faith and goodness, what message does that give to Christians going through tough times? What does Job recognize as the flaw of that doctrine? See Job 9:30-31, Psalm 51:5, Romans 8:1-23, Ephesians 2:8&9.

_____

_____

_____

_____

_____

9. Why, like Zophar, do we often resort to the *ad hominem* argument? See Job 11:1-8. What does Zophar teach us about making assumptions on why others suffer, or react negatively to their afflictions? See Job 11:13&14 in contrast to Job 1:1-3, 5, 8, and Job 2:3.

_____

_____

10. Why do we have to be careful not to rush to judgment? See Job 13:1&2. How should we respond when others come to tell us who we are, why we are in our struggles, and how we should fix things? See Job 22:5&6. See also how Moses responded to Miriam and Aaron's critique in Numbers 14.

11. How does Job find the Jesus of the gospel in his ash heap suffering? See Job 6:23 and 19:25. What do you think about his statement in Job 13:15? Do you see any connection to that and what Jesus calls us to commit to if we are going to be his fully devoted followers? See Matthew 6:24.

"Passions may
may imagine
vain things; b
shall still hav
word in every
and the casti
every decisio

rage...desires
all sorts of
it judgment
e the last
argument,
g vote on
"

Charlotte Bronte

Act Three: Scene One

THE LAST
WORD

FOR THE BETTER PART OF a day, Job has tried to justify himself. In the process, he has found fault with God. Yet in the nick of time he has pulled back from the edge of the abyss and integrity has won the day. His three comforters have fought him tooth and nail. The four old debaters have finally argued themselves into exhaustion. The silence is almost eerie. It can't end this way. Every story has to have some concluding words.

If all the world's a stage, and every person a player, the significance of our brief hour on the stage is in the final words. Otherwise, Shakespeare's Macbeth is right: "...it is a tale told by an idiot, full of sound and fury, signifying nothing."

You can tell a lot about people by their last words. On his deathbed, the Renaissance poet Francois Rabelais gasped out as his final words of unbelief: "I go to seek the Great Perhaps." Ludwig Beethoven joked, *Plaudite, amici, comedia finte est.* —"Applaud, my friends, the comedy is over." Leonardo di Vinci passed away with regret on his lips: "I have offended God and mankind because my work did not reach the quality it should."

We might all wish that we could go to our Maker with the words of Sydney Carton, the drunkard who experienced redemption in Charles Dickens' *Tale of Two Cities*. As he stood at the guillotine, having heroically traded places with the husband of the woman he loved, he said, "It is a far, far better thing that I do, than I have ever done; it is a far, far better rest that I go to than I have ever known."

Yet we are not the ones who pronounce the final judgment on our brief moment on life's stage. Those who remember us with kind eulogies are as flawed as our worst critics. Neither our friends nor our enemies know what God knows about us. He has the last word, and it is infallible.

ELIHU SETS THE STAGE

The young man has sat silent in the shadows. Middle Eastern Culture demands that Elihu sit quietly by in deference to his elders. He should be commended for holding his tongue so long. When the opening finally comes, his pent-up frustrations explode:

> "Inside I am like bottled-up wine, like wineskins
> ready to burst. I must speak and find relief..."
> —Job 32:19&20

There are good reasons to believe that Elihu is God's anointed spokesman. The Semitic name Elihu literally means "God is he." A variation could be "God is in him." He says of the speech that he is about to deliver, "...it is the spirit in a person, the breath of the Almighty, that gives them understanding." (Job 32:8) He adds,

"...the spirit within me compels me..." (Job 32:18) Old men at the ash heap speak from worldly experience and years of theological reflection. The young man can only find words given by the Holy Spirit. Later, when God appears to give the final pronouncement, he faults Job and rebukes Eliphaz, Zophar, and Bildad. Yet he does not criticize Elihu.

God seldom speaks to us directly. Most often, he uses people to deliver his message. We are right to listen to the sage advice of those like Job, Eliphaz, Bildad, and Zophar who have walked with God for many years. Their guidance is usually the most credible.

But sometimes God speaks through the young, the inexperienced, and even the foolish. St. Paul wrote, "God chose the foolish things of this world to shame the wise..." (1 Corinthians 1:27) Don't discount this Spirit-filled young man overshadowed by his elders on the stage. He is about to deliver a word straight from God.

A Challenge to Job

Eliphaz challenges the man on the ash heap by asserting that God is all wise. Though we may fault him for the way he deals with us, our reasoning is too feeble to comprehend the infinite mind of the Creator. "For God is greater than any mortal." (Job 33:12) After the greatest sages of the ages have exhausted their collective intelligence, they will barely have scratched the surface of the Divine's wisdom.

St. Augustine tells of the time he walked along the beach trying to figure out the mysteries of the Trinity. His head was about to explode. Then he saw a little boy digging a hole in the sand of the North African shoreline. He watched the boy carry seashells full of water from the Mediterranean to fill his hole.

"What are you doing?" asked the venerable saint. "Why, I am filling my hole with the sea," replied the lad. "Silly boy," thought Augustine as he walked away. Then it hit him like a thunderbolt: "I am that silly boy if I think that I can fill the finite hole of my mind with the infinite ocean of an inscrutable God." Elihu would have said "Amen!" to St. Augustine's confession.

The young man also challenges Job's complaint about God's capricious use of power. He counters that God has the sovereign right do as he wills with his creation and its creatures. Elihu would agree with the words of the Psalmist: "The earth is the LORD's, and all it contains, the world and those who dwell in it." (Psalm 24:1) It is a universal law that those who create something also own it. Elihu would also concur with St. Paul's assertion that God's people are twice-owned, first because he created us and then because he redeemed us in Christ: "...you are not your own, for you have been bought with a price." (1 Corinthians 6:19&20)

In the thirty-third chapter of Job's story, Elihu gives a harrowing list of the terrors that God may visit upon us. He can build us up and tear us down as he wishes. It is his right to give and take as he chooses. Job was right when he early rebuked his wife's complaint: "Shall we accept good from God, and not trouble?" (Job 2:10) Yet a year of unending calamity has eroded this suffering saint's ability to affirm God's right to yield power that causes dismay and distress. Elihu gives a soaring defense of the fact that God is both all powerful and all good:

1 God Uses His Power for Ultimate Good

If he gives us a season on the ash heap of affliction, it is only to shape us for a better future. Elihu describes some of the worst things that can possibly happen to us, and then says, "God does these things to a person—maybe once, even three times—to turn them back from the pit, that the light of life may shine on them." (Job 33:29&30)

2 God Is Shaping Us for Glory

Elihu's argument is a mirror image of what St. Paul says some 2,000 years later: "For our light and momentary troubles are achieving for us an eternal glory that far outweighs them all." (2 Corinthians 4:17) How can we say that Job's troubles were light? Paul would answer that they were in comparison to the infinite weight of glory yet to come. We might ask how Job's endless days and nights of trouble were momentary? Paul would smile and respond that they were short in contrast to the endless eternity still to come. To all this Elihu would shout, "Amen, brother Paul!"

3 God Protects Us While He's Shaping Us

Elihu says to Job that God doesn't leave the afflicted defenseless: "Yet there is an angel at their side, a messenger, one in a thousand sent to tell them how to be upright." (Job 33:23) God may have pulled back the hedge and allowed the dark angel to go on a rampage, but he also sent other angels to protect Job from the worst that Satan could do. Like the man from Uz, we sometimes feel that we can't bear another moment of pain and distress. We complain that God has abandoned us to our version of black leprosy. Yet Elihu would agree with St. Paul: "...God is faithful. He will not allow you to be tempted beyond what you can bear..." (1 Corinthians 10:13). He will give you supernatural grace to bear your pain. If it is finally too much, he will snatch you off the ash heap before the devil can steal your soul.

4 God Stays With Us During the Shaping Times

Those of us who have ever spent a season on the ash heap will testify that the most damnable aspect is the feeling that God is far away, uncaring, and silent in the face of our desperate prayers. Yet Elihu says, "That person can pray and find favor with him..." (Job 33:26) The fact that God is silent means that he is right beside us listening. Silence may be the best proof of empathy. The one who talks incessantly while we suffer is little or no help. True comforters silently observe and ponder, waiting for the perfect time to offer the best kind of help. God does the same.

5 God's Grace Isn't Based on Fairness

When Elihu tells Job that we "find favor with him," he uses a Hebrew word for favor that is synonymous with the New Testament word grace. Elihu's theology is repeated by a New Testament writer: "Let us then approach God's throne of grace with confidence, so that we might find mercy and grace to help us in the time of need." (Hebrews 4:16) Mercy and grace are not the same. Mercy is when we don't get the punishment we deserve. Grace is when we do get the blessings we don't deserve.

When bad things happen to good people, it won't be long before folks protest that God is unfair. Elihu would argue that this is the most illogical charge leveled against God. If God were really fair, and gave us exactly what we deserved, we would all be doomed. We should be thankful for the truth written by the Psalmist a thousand years after Elihu spoke: "God does not treat us as our sins deserve, or repay us according to our iniquities." (Psalm 103:10)

Bob Harrington was proclaimed the Chaplain of Bourbon Street, that New Orleans strip of neon lights and depravity. The

Reverend Harrington ministered to prostitutes, strip club dancers, drunks and derelicts. He tells about a time when he was praying with a Mafia capo that he had led to Christ. The mobster was minutes away from going into a courtroom where he would be sentenced for crimes he had committed. The chaplain put his arms around the converted Mafioso and prayed, "Lord, please give my dear brother justice today." The convicted gangster frantically interrupted his prayer, "I don't want justice. Pray that the judge will give me mercy!" If God were fair, we would all be as doomed as that hoodlum.

Instead, God is *super* fair. Anything he gives us is way beyond fair. We deserve hell. If we are given life, it is more than we deserve. If we get life plus anything else, it is far beyond anything we merit. If he gives us heaven too, then we are recipients of amazing grace. I have a friend who always has the same answer when anyone asks how he's doing. He smiles and says, "Better than I deserve." If we can say that, and really mean it, then no ash heap experience will cause us to say with Job, "God hasn't been fair to me."

Elihu has unfolded a soaring doxology to the God who is all wise, all powerful, and all good. The young man boldly says to his suffering elder, "Pay attention, Job, and listen to me..." (Job 33:31) Elihu might as well be speaking to all of us who have crowded into The Theater of Angels. This is our God too, whether we are in times of plenty or on the ash heap of affliction. He must be embraced as even *mega* fair, regardless of our circumstances.

A Word to Job's Comforters

Elihu now confronts Job's buddies: "Hear my words, you wise men; listen to me you men of learning." (Job 34:2). No matter how much knowledge we have attained through book learning or life experience, we have not learned it all. It is possible to be an educated idiot. Real wisdom is always ready to listen and learn something new. Old men can even learn from a young whippersnapper.

Elihu's second speech lasts a staggering four chapters (Job 34-37) A surface reading would seem to be a rehash of arguments already advanced against Job by Eliphaz, Bildad, and Zophar. But there is a fundamental difference: they focused on what was wrong with Job's attitude and theology while Elihu focuses on what is right with Job's God. He teaches us that we don't need to defend God. The Most High has not called us to convince others or batter them into submission. The work of changing minds and transforming lives belongs exclusively to the Holy Spirit.

The three older comforters got angry at Job because he didn't see things their way. They took his rebuff of their words as a repudiation of truth and a rejection of them. Elihu is passionate, but not overbearing. He admits, "I am young in years and you are old...I was fearful, not daring to tell you what I know." (Job 32:6) Right from the beginning he asks for permission to speak and makes a humble appeal: "But please, Job, hear my words." (Job 33:1) The three older comforters showed little humility or compassion. After four hours of heated debate they proved that clarity without comfort is of little value when it comes to making things better.

In the 34th chapter, he challenges Job's complaint that God withheld justice. He again deals with the issue of fairness. The laws of reaping and sowing are inviolate. The wicked are ultimately punished and the righteous will finally be blessed. God isn't obligated to execute his judgments in our way or according to our timetable. The fact that his ways are beyond us only proves that we aren't smart enough to figure them out or pass judgment on them.

Elihu asks, "If he [God] remains silent, who can condemn him? If he hides his face, who can find him?" (Job 34:29) He then asks a question of all of us who call God's fairness into question: "Should God reward you on your terms when you refuse to repent?" (Job 34:33) In short, would it be better to put the management of justice in the hands of the unrepentant? Do you think that finite sinners have a better idea of who to reward or who to punish? Would you rather trust them to mete out the right kind of rewards or punishment, or would it be better to trust in the Lord's wisdom, his ways, and his timetable? Again, Elihu's response is vastly superior to those of the elder comforters because its focus is on the goodness of God rather than the badness of Job's complaints.

The young man ratchets up his argument in the 35th chapter. It is compelling in its simplicity: "If you are righteous, what do you give to him, or what does he receive from your hand?" (Job 35:7) This question is devastating in the light of our constant questioning of how God handles our affairs. If we know better than our Lord, what have we ever done to prove our competence? Certainly, history is littered with the wreckage of humanity's futile attempts to improve things. We destroy economies, pollute environments, and ruin lives. In the past 6,000 years there has only been 270 years without war on planet earth. We strive to create utopia while marching inexorably toward Armageddon. Like Job, we multiply words about the problems of a broken world, but we have not proven that we can fix it without creating more complications. (Job 35:16)

Elihu soars in the 36th chapter, composing a breathtaking symphony in praise of God's goodness: God is mighty, but he doesn't look down his nose at anyone (Job 36:7); he will repay the wicked in his good time, and exalt the righteous when he is ready (Job 36:8); he will give the afflicted every chance to learn from the suffering so that they will become better through it (Job 36:9-11); yet he will not allow the unrepentant evildoer and deceptive hypocrite to continue to bully the oppressed indefinitely (Job 36:12-11); at the perfect time he will raise the oppressed from the dust and lead them to the banquet table of his riches (Job 36:15&16). As he surveys the goodness of God, Elihu asks, "Who can say to him, 'You have done wrong?' (Job 36:23)

But Elihu is not yet done with his grand oratorio of praise. He looks at the lower order of God's creatures: the beasts of the field. They have no souls or eternal future. They will be slaughtered for food or plowed into the earth as fertilizer. Yet God cares for them too (Job 36:33) Elihu prefigures the words of Jesus 2,000 years later:

> "Look at the birds of the air; they do not sow or
> reap or store away in barns, and yet your heavenly
> Father feeds them. Are you not much more
> valuable than they?"
>
> —*Matthew 6:26*

His grand composition of praise reaches its crescendo in the 37th chapter with soaring lyrics: "At this my heart pounds and leaps from its place." (Job 37:1) Elihu sings of God's magnificent governance of the universe, of seasons, rains that nourish the earth, snowfalls that fill rivers, ice fields and deserts, the cycles of animal life, and how everything works in perfect harmony for the good of creation and its creatures.

He pleads with the man from Uz to look beyond the ash heap of his own suffering: "Stop and consider his wonders." (Job 37:14) He reminds Job, and all the afflicted in every age, of the danger of allowing our pain to make us go inward and narcissistic. In our self-focus, our soul is made smaller, our eyes dimmer, and our view of life so much narrower.

Elihu brings his masterpiece of praise to its final notes by declaring God's excellence (Job 37:23). Such wisdom, power, and goodness, all blended together in perfect harmony, begs the most compelling question of all: shouldn't we revere him rather than fear him? (Job 37:23&24)

When the Ash Heap becomes a Cathedral

Elihu has unmasked Job as one who has allowed afflictions to take his eyes off God, and his comforters for letting Job's attitudes and faulty thinking take their focus off the Most High too. When we focus on problems rather than praise, difficulties seem to grow bigger and our Lord appears to get smaller.

When our problems weigh us down, it might help to look at this page of biblical history: A remnant of ancient Jews had returned from Babylonian captivity to rebuild the broken walls of Jerusalem. The work was overwhelming and their enemies were determined to stop them. The governor of Jerusalem gave them this remedy for their despair: "Do not grieve, for the joy of the LORD is your strength." (Nehemiah 8:10) He ordered them to go home, celebrate God's goodness with feasting and praise songs, and then come back to restore broken walls with refreshed souls and renewed strength.

We shouldn't minimize the devastations that bombarded Job. Elihu never trivialized the man's sufferings. Yet a continued focus on them didn't make his time on the ash heap any better. Young Elihu is right: There comes a time when we need to stop grieving and start praising. Job needs to return to worshipping God the way he did at his children's gravesite. Refocusing on the greatness of God, as Elihu has just done, makes our problems so much smaller by comparison. Even though we might be sitting bloodied and soot-covered on our ash heap, if we will lift up the hands of a leper to the heavens in praise, the promise of Psalm 30:5 just might come true sooner than we think: "Weeping lasts for a night, but joy comes in the morning."

GOD DELIVERS THE LAST WORD

The last note of Elihu's great praise song ends. There is only a moment of awed silence before a sudden dust storm begins to howl and swirl around Job's ash heap. We read, "Then the LORD spoke to Job out of the storm..." (Job 38:1) We shouldn't miss the profound lesson here. Throughout his year of black leprosy, Job has repeatedly cried out to God. The Most High has responded with silence. Job has often voiced the lament of the afflicted: "Where is God when it hurts?" God does not appear when Job weeps. Nor does he come when he complains. Neither does he show up during the theological debate between four angry old men. But he does appear when Elihu sings his praises. King David made a profound theological statement when he sang to God, "You are enthroned on the praises of Israel." (Psalm 22:3)

If we want to rise up from our ash heap affliction, we must give ourselves to praise even when our heart is breaking. When he was going through one of the most trying times of his life,

David wrote this line in another of his praise songs: "Take delight in the LORD, and he will give you the desires of your heart." (Psalm 37:4) It is not by accident that God finally shows up during the closing notes of Elihu's great praise song.

God's Word to Job

We want God to break his silence with words of comfort. Yet sometimes he stings us with a rebuke. Throughout his complaints on the ash heap, Job has been calling God out. Now God shows up to take on Job's challenge. The man on the ash heap must be petrified when he sees the Most High clothed in the fury of a whirlwind. A voice bellows out in the howling of gale force winds: "Brace yourself like a man!" (Job 38:3) God is using the language of the boxing ring: "Put up your dukes, and get ready to take me on. I'm about to come after you with some heavy body blows."

The Super Heavyweight Champion of the Universe moves with lightning quick speed, peppering Job with fifty-three rapid fire questions in a row. They all have to do with running the cosmos. Can Job put the macrocosms of solar systems together so that they can hum through the vastness of interstellar space with uninterrupted precision? Can he keep the stars in their orbit, the planets spinning, or the seasons revolving in their endless cycles? (Job 38:3-35) Job's mind must be spinning from the opening salvo: "Where were you when I laid the earth's foundations?" (Job 38:4)

The Creator jumps from macrocosms to microcosms. Not only did he set the intricate movements of the galaxies, he designed the microscopic DNA strands of the human brain. He taunts Job even as he jabs away, "Who has given wisdom to the mind? Or who has given understanding to the heart?" (Job 38:36 *KJV*)

Job doesn't even have time to counterpunch in response to this dizzying barrage of questions before God takes him on a trip to the zoo. The Most High fires off twenty-nine more lightning quick questions about lions, mountain goats, donkeys, wild oxen, ostriches, war horses, and hawks. Again he dances around the ring taunting a punch drunk fighter: If Job can question God's way of managing his life, surely the man from Uz must know how to manage the animal kingdom, as well as stars in the galaxies and weather on planet earth.

What the arguments of Job's comforters couldn't do, God achieves. Job is pummeled into submission. He can only respond, "I am unworthy. How can I reply to you? I put my hand over my mouth...I have no answers..." (Job 40:4&5) Yet God isn't done. Job is about to receive more body blows from what Oswald Chambers called, "God's severe mercy." Again he warns his staggering opponent in the ring: "Brace yourself like a man." (Job 40:7)

Job is peppered with more questions as the Most High moves from his wisdom to his power. He speaks of two massive and mysterious creatures that the King James Version of the Bible call the behemoth and the leviathan. The description of these beasts in Job's story are compatible with everything we know about dinosaurs and prehistoric water monsters that roamed the world, not millions of years as some have suggested, but maybe even thousands of years ago. God asks Job if he could handle such monsters in his own strength, let alone create them, fill the earth with them, and then cause them to go extinct. These questions are surely designed to strip any remaining vestiges of arrogance from Job.

We are reminded of the famous World Championship Middle Weight fight between Sugar Ray Leonard and Roberto Durán on

November 25, 1980. In the closing seconds of the eighth round, a badly beaten Durán waved Leonard off and said to the referee, *No Más!* –"No more!" Job waves God off with the Semitic equivalent of *No Más!* He cries out, "My ears have heard of you, but now my eyes have seen you. Therefore, I despise myself in dust and ashes." (Job 42:4-6)

When other people try to convince us of biblical truth, it has little effect. When God's Spirit reveals himself in all his glory, we finally see ourselves as we really are. We are not wise enough to question his wisdom. We are not powerful enough to challenge his power. We are not good enough to dispute his goodness. We can only fall down in repentance for our foolishness, and praise him for his amazing grace.

God's Last Word to Job's Comforters

Eliphaz, Bildad, and Zophar can take no delight in the confession that they had worked all day to beat out of Job. The words of Jesus now come home to roost:

> "Do not judge others, or you too will be judged.
> For in the same way you judge others, you will
> be judged, and with the measure you use, it will
> be measured to you."
>
> *—Matthew 7:1&2*

The whirlwind of fury that has reduced Job to utter humility now turns on his three buddies. God says to Eliphaz, "I am angry with you and your two friends, because you have not spoken the truth about me as my servant Job has." (Job 42:7) At first glance, these words are difficult to understand. If we look back at the ash heap debate, their theology seems like solid biblical orthodoxy. They actually defended God while Job complained about him.

Maybe the key to God's rebuke of these three is found in that little phrase, "...my servant Job..." Is God saying that these comforters were not acting as his servants when they were trying to set Job straight? Is it possible to deceive ourselves into thinking that we are doing God's work when we are actually promoting ourselves? We say that we are defending God's reputation, but are we really promoting our own theological positions? We piously claim that we are trying to help others for the sake of God, but are we grandstanding for our own glory? So much of what passes for God's work is often done to accomplish our own agenda.

These three accused Job of arrogance. They are just as arrogant. The difference is that the man who sits on the ash heap has repented while they sit on a dung heap of their own doctrinal smugness. Is it any wonder that Jesus often preferred the honest prostitute to the disingenuous Pharisee? One thinks of Jesus' parable about the despicable tax collector and the religious bigot. The tax collector is a traitor to his country and a mobster who takes food out of the mouths of hungry children.

The religious Pharisee fastidiously keeps Torah Law. The two end up in the same temple. However, their prayers are as different as night and day. The tax collector weeps for his sin, pounds on his chest, and cries out in repentance. The Pharisee shakes his head in disgust that the tax collector should even be allowed in the holy temple, and then thanks God that he is not like that scoundrel. Christ's story ends with these sobering lines:

"I tell you that this man [the tax collector], rather than the other [the Pharisee] went home justified

before God. All those who exalt themselves will
be humbled, and those who humble themselves
will be exalted."

—*Luke 18:14*

There is only one solution for these three. God tells them that they must offer up a sacrifice. (Job 42:8) Don't miss the delicious irony of this moment. These religious men, steeped in correct orthodoxy, need the same blood of the Lamb to wash away their sins as did the wayward sons and daughters of Job. This is a sobering reminder to all of us who put too much trust in our biblical theology and then feel superior to those who fall short of our orthodoxy. We all stand equally as sinners before the cross of Christ. When King David considered all the sacrifices that he might bring to God, he concluded, "My sacrifice, O God, is a broken spirit; a broken and contrite heart, God, you will not despise." (Psalm 51:17)

A heart of humility, broken by the awful awareness of one's own sin, is what most pleases the Most High. God's final word on Job's comforters is that their lofty theology was accompanied by proud hearts. Sometimes that's why it is better to be on the ash heap than to be sitting next to it.

God surely disciplines those he loves. We might even say that those God royally elects, he ruthlessly perfects. Dear friend, we all need the severe mercy of God. We might be the ash heap sufferer who allows self-pity to steal our gratitude and worship. Or we could be the sincere comforter who allows our orthodoxy to lead us into the pride of our own religious self-sufficiency. If God disciplines us it is because he loves us. Whether we are on the ash heap, or sitting beside it, he is all about conforming all his redeemed sons and daughters into the image of his beloved Son. Dear friend, let's take a moment and thank God for those times when he tears off our fig leaves and masks to reveal the truth about us. Without those times we would never grow up.

But Joy *Does* Come in the Morning

Stick around for the final scene. The best is yet to come. After sitting through the ash heap season, you don't want to miss the Happily-Ever-After ending in The Theater of Angels.

STORIES
SET IN STONE

A STUDY GUIDE

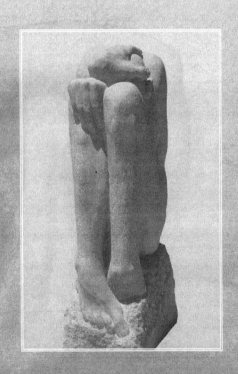

Claudia's Job has his feet dug in. His back is contorted, and shoulders raised in defense. Job's head is lowered in shame but also arched in unbroken stubbornness. His right hand is clasped over his right knee to keep from kneeling in worship or standing up to move on. One sees a petulant child who refuses to submit, squeezed into a narrow box of self-pity. His posture is all the more defensive after the brutal and unfair assault of his comforters.

He desperately needs to get out of the box. He requires a friend who will give him tough love that turns his eyes from self to God, from pity to praise. Only then will God come to bring the healing he craves. The same is true for us. May the following questions serve to that end for each of us.

1. What do you think of the statement:, "Those who remember us with kind eulogies are as flawed as our worst critics?" Why is God's assessment the only one that matters? See 1 Samuel 16:7, 1 Chronicles 20:9, Psalm 139:1, 23&24, Jeremiah 17:10.

    _____

    _____

    _____

    _____

    _____

    _____

2. Why is Elihu the most credible comforter? What does the young man do right that his elders did wrong? See Job 32:6-9, 32:18, 33:1 & 33:1-7.

    _____

    _____

3.   What do you think of Elihu's repudiation of Job's charges that God is unfair in his dealings? Review and comment on them:

God uses his power for ultimate good. See Job 33:29&30, Psalm 103:10, 2 Corinthians 14:15-17, Hebrews 4:6.

God is shaping us for his glory. See Job 33:29&30, 3 Corinthians 4:17, Ephesians 2:10.

God protects us while he shapes us. See Job 33:23, I Corinthians 10:13, Hebrews 7:25.

God stays with us in the shaping times. See Job 33:26, Matthew 28:20, Romans 8:26&27, 2 Corinthians 12:9.

Grace isn't based on fairness. See again Job 33:26, also Psalm 103:10, Ephesians 2:8&9. What do we really deserve? Do we really want God to be fair? What about *super* fair?

4. Though Elihu rehashes his elders' arguments (see Job 34-37), what's the difference? In **tone**? See Job 32:6-33:7. In **focus**? Notice they focused on Job's shortcomings while he pointed to God's greatness. See Job 36. In his **joyful enthusiasm**? See Job 37:1. In **Job's response**? Notice Job was silent and not defensive. When treated with respect, he listened. When Elihu was not defensive or argumentative, neither was Job. What do you learn from all of this?

    _____

    _____

    _____

    _____

    _____

    _____

    _____

5. What do you think about the author's insight that God didn't come until after Elihu's praise service? See also 2 Chronicles 7:1, Psalm 22:3 & 37:4, Isaiah 6:1-4, and Acts 4:31.

    _____

    _____

    _____

    _____

    _____

    _____

6. Do you like the way God finally showed up? We often say that we want God to come in all his glory. What if he really did? See Job 38:2-3, Job 37:22, Isaiah 6:5, Hebrews 10:31.

7. What are God's answers to Job's complaints? See Job 38:3-35 as a snapshot. What was Job's response? See Job 40:4&5 and 42:4-6. Is this what Oswald Chambers calls the severe mercy of God? What do you feel about God's dealing with Job?

8. What do you learn from God's short rebuke of Job's comforters? See Job 42:7. What do you learn about yourself in this rebuke? See Matthew 7:1-2 and Luke 8:24. Do you find it ironic that the defenders of orthodoxy needed the same blood sacrifice as Job's wayward kids? See Job 42:8. What does that say to you?

" Happily-ever
come in happ
days. They ar
end of challe
met, promise
and tears-eve

afters don't
ly-every-
found at the
ges-ever-
-ever-kept,
-wept. "

Richelle Goodrich

Act Three: Scene Two

EVER AFTER

THE COWBOY RIDES OFF INTO the sunset. Superman saves Gotham city again. Cinderella gets Prince Charming. Indiana Jones escapes the Temple of Doom. Rocky Balboa goes the distance. We love a happy ending. Some books, plays, and movies leave us hanging at the end. But The Theater of Angels never leaves the audience dangling. Heaven's Playwright has a good purpose. Remember St. Paul's words:

> "His intent was that now, through the church, the
> manifold wisdom of God should be made known
> to the rulers and authorities in the heavenly realms
> according to his eternal purpose..."
>
> *--Ephesians 3:10&11*

Every presentation at The Theater of Angels must have a happy ending. God will be proven to be all wise, all powerful, and all good. Heroes will always win, damsels in distress will be forever rescued, villains will invariably lose, good will triumph

THE THEATER OF ANGELS

every time, and redemption will complete its work before the final curtain falls.

Job's Happily Ever After

Nowhere is God's happy ending more evident than in the final scene in Job's story. It begins with that oft-quoted line:

> "And the LORD restored Job's losses...indeed, the
> LORD gave Job twice as much as he had before."
>
> —*Job 42:10*

The Psalmist said, "Weeping lasts for a night, but joy comes in the morning." (Psalm 30:5) Sometimes weeping lasts for several nights. In Job's case it probably lasted for a year. Nevertheless, the season of suffering for God's people is just that: a *season*, not an endless eternity. Tough times never last, but God's goodness does. After he tore down the hedges that had protected a godless Israel, allowing a plague of locusts to strip the land bare, God promised his prophet: "I will restore to you the years that the swarming locusts have eaten..." (Joel 2:25) The God who takes away, always gives back so much more. In Job's case it was double what he took.

A Better Righteousness

The script says, "After Job prayed for his friends, the LORD restored his fortunes and gave him twice as much as he had before." (Job 42:10) Notice that the restored fortune comes *after* Job prays for his friends. It couldn't have been easy for him to intercede with God to forgive his comforters after the way they abused him at the ash heap. Before God revealed himself in the whirlwind, Job angrily condemned his buddies for their accusations. He judged them just as harshly as they judged him. Their ash heap debate was tit-for-tat nastiness.

Before his time on the ash heap, Job was famously righteous. He fastidiously shunned evil. Yet he did it because he feared God's punishment for sin. His many attempts to justify his righteousness to his friends during the ash heap debate proved that he gloried in his personal integrity. He showed that he trusted too much in his own goodness. He assumed that his godliness would spare him from affliction. He bellyached that he deserved better from God than what he got.

Now he has a better righteousness. He understands grace. The ash heap has stripped away his pride. It has made him more empathetic of human frailty, including that of his three friends. He can now forgive them, and pray to a gracious God to accept their sacrifices. Job has received double of all that he lost, but he received something far more valuable: a double-portion of transforming grace that trumps all the righteousness than he ever had before.

Better Riches

Job would never want to repeat that ash heap experience again, but he probably wouldn't have taken anything for the blessings he received as a result. His fortune is suddenly doubled from what it was a year before. By any measure, that's not a bad year's return! He now has double the sheep, camels, oxen, and donkeys (Job 42:12) Once again he's cornered the stock market in Uz.

Better Family

Job gets seven new sons and three daughters. (Job 42:13) Nothing will ever replace the children that he lost in the tornado, but he has the joy of fatherhood again. We shouldn't gloss over the fact that he got a new and improved wife. Whereas she was once angry and bitter, making up excuses to stay away from her ash heap man, she is now in love with him again. Their restored passion produces ten children. Maybe Mrs. Job experienced a renewed love for her husband because he has been made better by his season of suffering. She too has seen that, though he may remove the protective hedges for a season, God always gives back far more than he takes away.

The new batch of kids are so much better than the first. We read nothing about wild parties, nor of Job having to make weekly sacrifices to atone for their bad behavior. His three daughters are the light of his life. In all the land of Uz there are no women more beautiful. (Job 42:15) He calls his first girl Jemimah, which means warm and affectionate. His second is Kesiah, the ancient Semitic name for sweet cinnamon powder. The third is Keren-Happuch, which means to shine with radiance. Taking these three names together, Job's three girls bring affection, sweetness, and radiance to his life. They are so dear to him that he does something almost unthinkable in ancient Middle Eastern culture when he gives each of them an equal inheritance to his sons. (Job 42:15)

Better Respect

Suddenly, the house that was empty during his ash heap days is filled with people again. (Job 42:11) Relatives that stayed away are now dropping in for dinner. Acquaintances who gave him the cold shoulder during his calamities are now sending engraved invitations to join their dinner parties. People who offered no comfort during his season of suffering are now telling him how sorry they were for his troubles. Job 42:11 says, "...and each one gave him a piece of silver and a gold ring." Maybe they were giving a kind of guilt offering to atone for their inexcusable neglect during his days of affliction.

It would have been understandable for Job to slam the door in their faces. At the very least, most of us might have given our fair-weather pals a stern lecture on friendship. But the ash heap has changed Job. Suffering has given him an uncommon empathy and grace. He welcomes them back without rancor.

The watching world can now respect Job, not for his blameless life, but even more for his gracious attitude. Before Job's calamity, we don't read that his house was full of people. Perhaps folks were intimidated by his success. But now they are drawn to his humility and hospitality. This is surely a new and improved Job.

A Long Life

During the dark night of his soul, Job's wife demanded that he curse God and die. There were many agonizing nights of black leprosy when he begged God to take his life and end his misery. He even complained that God was cruel in letting him hang on. But God knows a future that we can never see from the vantage point of our ash heap. The Most High knew that beyond the winter of Job's discontent a springtime would blossom into unparalleled prosperity.

You can bet that Job now breathes a sigh of relief that God didn't answer his ash heap prayers. Look at all he would have missed had God given him what he pleaded for during those dark days of limited perspective. Some of God's greatest gifts to us are unanswered prayers.

Job lives one hundred and forty more years after his ash heap experience. (Job 42:16) He not only has the joy of raising seven honorable sons and three beautiful daughters, he gets to romp with a passel of grandkids. But Job 42:16 says that he gets four generations of grandchildren which would include great grandchildren, great-great grandchildren, and great-great-great grandchildren.

The possibilities are staggering. If each of his descendants would have birthed the same number of children that Job and his wife produced, the number of offspring in his lifetime could have numbered ten thousand! Yes, the Lord does take away. Job knew that full well when he lay prostrate on the graves of his first children. Yet the Lord gives so much more than he ever takes away.

We come to the final line of Job's great drama: "And so he died, an old man and full of days." (Job 42:17) "Full of days" means more than the number of his years. It is a grand statement about the fullness of those years. There was a year from hell. But that was balanced off by all the years of blessing before, and 140 years of greater blessings afterwards. Indeed, God is all wise! He is all powerful! He is all good!

A Distant Happily Ever After

Yet we have to be careful not to read too much into the blessings that were lavished on Job after his stint on the ash heap. It would be tempting to extrapolate from this story that we can expect to reap double in worldly success as a reward for going through tribulations. This kind of shallow prosperity gospel does not hold up to the scrutiny of Scripture. The ash heap does not always yield double bonus points.

The Quid Pro Quo of a "seed faith" prosperity gospel advanced by some unscrupulous televangelists sets the naïve up for disappointment, and even disillusionment. When Rabbi Harold Kushner buried his son after he died of progeria, it broke his heart and shattered his faith. God didn't give him two more sons to take that boy's place. The number of the afflicted who never saw the sun rise again on their lives is significant.

Some might argue that Kushner never got blessed like Job because he refused to see God as all wise, all powerful, and all good in the aftermath of his tragedy. Some Christians might even pompously suggest that if this Jewish rabbi would come to Jesus, he would experience Job-sized blessings.

Yet the Scripture is filled with saints who went to their graves stripped of everything. The eleventh chapter of the New Testament book of Hebrews is often called God's Hall of Fame. In this chapter, the names of God's greatest faith heroes are inscribed: champions like Abel, Abraham, Moses, Gideon, Samuel, David, and Rahab. The list ends with Jesus Christ in the 12th chapter of Hebrews. As you walk through these hallowed halls, you are inspired by the awesome feats of faith recorded on the plaques that line the walls. Yet at the end of the hallway, there is a final statement etched over the exit door:

"These were all commended for their faith, yet none of them received what had been promised, since God had planned something better for us so that only together with us would they be made perfect."

—Hebrews 11:39&40

A single phrase on that inscription is shocking: "...yet not one of them received what had been promised..." Let those words sink in: "...not one of them..." They went to their graves unrewarded in this life. The eleventh chapter of Hebrews also lists nameless heroes who went about in animal skins, living in holes in the ground, hounded as fugitives, and then dying agonizing deaths as martyrs. Their Happily Ever After did not come this side of heaven, but in a glory that comes on the other side of the grave. (Hebrews 11:40) This ability to look beyond this life for our reward requires that we live by faith.

Hebrews 11:1 says, "Now faith is confidence in what we hope for and assurance of what we do not see." God may choose to give us double-blessings as he gave Job, but this is no certainty. We must always look beyond our ash heap to a more distant Happily Ever After. There we will see our Redeemer in the land of the living where his resurrected followers live, not for Job's 140 more years—but forever.

Lazarus' Distant Happily Ever After

One of Jesus' most beloved stories is about a rich man and a beggar. (Luke 16:19-31) Lazarus is Hebrew for "God is my help." He surely needed God's help because no one else ever came to his aid. He eked out his miserable existence on the mean streets outside a rich man's mansion. There he sat on his ash heap day after day, begging for his daily bread.

Like Job, he was covered with running sores and stinking to the high heavens. This bag of bones shook his beggar's bowl in the face of everyone who passed by, but they held their noses and pretended not to see him. He longed for the table scraps from the rich man's table, but got none of them. His only comfort in life was the street dogs that came to lick his sores. Only a good God would have put it in the hearts of ravenous dogs to lick his sores instead of attacking and devouring him.

It is a delectable irony that both Lazarus and the rich man died on the same night. Jesus wants us to know that death plays no favorites. All the wealth in the world can't keep the final curtain falling at its appointed time.

The carcass of the beggar is thrown on the garbage pile. The rich man is given an opulent funeral attended by society's elite who praise him to the high heavens. No one remembers Lazarus, or even cares that there is one less beggar on the streets. Yet, in the heavenly realms, the tables are reversed. Even as the clods of dirt from the gravedigger's shovel are thundering down on his mahogany coffin lid, the rich man screams in an agony never experienced by the beggar. An ash heap would have been preferable to the flames of Hades where he now writhes in unquenchable thirst.

In this life he reaped the double portion of Job, even though he ignored God. Sometimes we are as distressed when good things happen to bad people as we are when bad things happen to good people. A good God will make his common grace available even to the wicked, but only for a short season in the light of an eternal hell.

Yet Lazarus never lost his hope in the goodness of God, even when he languished in beggar's rags. He would have given anything to enjoy leftovers from the rich man's table, but he was willing to hold out for a distant Happily Ever After. There must have been days and nights of suffering that seemed to drag on forever, but Lazarus' afflictions were light and momentary compared to the weight of eternal glory that was awaiting him. Now the former beggar snuggles in the arms of Father Abraham. His blessing is infinitely greater than the double portion of Job, and for infinitely longer than a mere 140 more years.

St. Paul's Distant Happily After

In a moment of transparency, the Apostle Paul tells about fourteen years of unending agony. (2 Corinthians 12:1-10) The Greek words that he uses to describe his sufferings are gut-wrenchingly graphic, and not for the faint of heart. He speaks of a "thorn in the flesh" that might better be translated as being impaled on a stake. As he slowly turns, the stake works its way with excruciating slowness through his innards. At the same time a demon beats on him with fists day and night. We may never know the exact affliction that he endured, but St. Paul's metaphors are disturbing enough.

He tells us that three times he pleaded with God to call off the demon and pull him off that sharpened stake. In the original language, these are not three quick prayers, but long seasons of desperate, around-the-clock wrestling with God. He uses Greek verbiage that describes coming to the snapping point. Imagine this superhero of the Christian Faith almost having a nervous breakdown!

Yet there came a point when he had to accept the inevitable: God wasn't going to take him off his ash heap of suffering. Most of us wouldn't want to hear the answer that Paul's Savior gave him: "My grace is sufficient for you, for my power is made perfect in weakness." (2 Corinthians 12:9) Sometimes God doesn't remove the affliction that forces us to depend on his grace. Yet, as we grow weaker, Christ grows stronger in us. Once St. Paul accepted this difficult truth, he was able to accept his suffering as a blessing:

> "Therefore, I will boast all the more gladly about my weakness, so that Christ's power may dwell in me."
>
> —2 Corinthians 12:9

Sometimes our Happily Ever After comes this side of heaven, but it isn't the sort of blessings that were given to Job. This Happily Ever After is even better: an ability to allow the afflictions of life not only to shape us, but to remain in us so that we can do so much more through Christ's power. This was the Happily Ever After that St. Paul found in his life. Perhaps nothing expresses this ash heap change of perspective more than a handwritten note found on the body of a dead Confederate soldier:

"I asked for strength that I might achieve.
I was made weak that I might learn humbly
  to obey.
I asked for health that I might do great things.
I was given infirmity that I might do better things.
I asked for riches that I might be happy.
I was given poverty that I might be wise.
I asked for power that I might feel the praise
  of men.
I was given weakness that I might feel the need
  of God.
I asked for all things that I might enjoy life.
I was given life that I might enjoy all things.
I got nothing that I asked for, but everything
  I hoped for.
And, almost despite myself, I am of all men
  most richly blessed."

St. Paul would say "Amen!" to that Confederate soldier's final prayer. Yet he knows that, though we can find joy and power in life on the ash heap, it still isn't the distant Happily Ever After.

There's so much more beyond the final curtain of life. One can only imagine what Paul thought when he bared his head to the executioner's blade in Nero's prison. Maybe he thought back to that line he had written in his second letter to the Corinthians:

> "For our light and momentary troubles are achieving for us an eternal glory that outweighs them all."
>
> —*2 Corinthians 4:17*

Our Distant Happily After

Do you remember when we were about to exit from God's Hall of Fame in the eleventh chapter of Hebrews? The writer of Hebrews wanted us to take one last look at that final inscription above the exit door: "God has planned something better for us..." (Hebrews 11:40) We have peeked behind the curtain of heaven that Job was never privileged to pull back. We have looked into the face of the Savior that Old Testament prophets could only see through distant mists. We have the full gospel that explains mysteries locked up to superheroes of old. We are filled with a Holy Spirit power that only fell occasionally and temporarily on them. Their sacrifices and religious rites could only prefigure the coming Messiah whose presence now dwells through the Holy Spirit within believers. Even if we languish on the ash heap, Jesus Christ sits alongside us as an infinitely truer and better comforter than Job's friends.

Job got a new and better family, but no matter how many years he got to enjoy them, a day came when he had to say goodbye. Yet we have a forever family made up from people of every tongue, tribe, and nation who will share a glorious and eternal future with us. Indeed, we have seen the Redeemer that Job could only see in shadows from a distance. Unlike Job, we do not have to wait to see him on the other side of the grave "in the land of the living." Through faith in Jesus Christ, we live with our Risen Redeemer in abundant life *this* side of the grave.

This story of Job gives us hope that weeping lasts for a night. During the long night of weeping we must never let go of optimism that a better day may come tomorrow. But more importantly, we must never lose confidence in that distant Happily Ever After. African American slaves used to call it "that great gettin' up morning"—a day when all of God's children will rise to meet our Redeemer in the air, be made gloriously like Jesus in the twinkling of an eye, and then live forever in a new heaven and earth.

The story of Lazarus reminds us that Job's second round of blessings may not come until we get to the other side of the grave and meet our Redeemer in the land of the living. Yet, when those blessings come, they will be infinitely better than anything Job got after his ash heap days.

St. Paul's triumph over afflictions teaches us that a new perspective can bring a spiritual Happily Ever After even if the tough times never go away in this life. Yet, a day is surely coming when our light and momentary sufferings will be exchanged for an eternal weight of glory in the distant and far better Happily Ever After.

This requires of us a deep and abiding faith that an all wise God knows better than all of us how to manage our personal lives, as well as the whole of his cosmos. This faith also rests in an enduring faith in an all-powerful God who is able to accomplish all his purposes. This faith never doubts that an all good God always works for the good of those who love him and are called according to his purpose. (Romans 8:28) To all this, Job, Jesus, Lazarus, St. Paul and millions of ash heap saints down through the corridors of time would say a hearty, "Amen!"

But it's not over Quite Yet

Now the curtain falls on Job's story for the last time. However, something is still missing. The biblical account ends without a mention of what happens to Satan and his emissaries from hell. How can we end a good story without dealing with the villain? Don't worry. We can find out what happened to Satan, if we will take the time to peek one last time behind the curtain. So stick around for an exclusive V.I.P. gathering designed to take you behind the scenes. In a moment, the venerable St. Paul will come out to finish the story.

If you don't mind, I would like to join him on stage to tell how my story is still playing out in The Theater of Angels. It is my sincerest hope that it will make you appreciate and celebrate your personal story all the more.

STORIES
SET IN STONE

A STUDY GUIDE

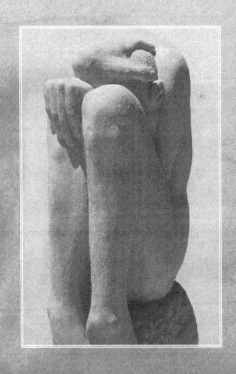

Claudia's Job captures only a moment in his life, forever frozen in stone. It is like a crucifix, both true and false at the same time. Christ did hang on that cross, but he is now the Risen Christ. Just as Christ is no longer on the cross, Job got off the ash heap. Tough times never last. Joy comes in the morning. Resurrection swallows up death, and we will all see our Redeemer in the land of the living. There is a Happily Ever After, both now and in a near distant time.

Claudia's Job has limitless potential to inspire us with awe. It also has its limits. It can't show Job before and after. And yet, his past is in that ash heap, and there is a sense in the stone that he will rise up to his full seven foot height and walk into a far better future. Let's talk together about Happily Ever After, both now and distant.

1. Is it true that every presentation on center stage in The Theater of Angels must have a happy ending? See. Job 42:10, Psalm 30:5, Joel 2:25, Romans 8:28, 2 Corinthians 4:17, Ephesians 3:10&11.

    _____

    _____

    _____

    _____

    _____

2. What do you make of the fact that Job's restoration came after he repented to God and forgave his comforters? See Job 42:40. Is it possible that we remain tied to the ash heap because we are harboring sins against God and bitterness towards others? Notice

that the Lord's prayer ends with a call for us to forgive others as God forgives us (Matthew 6:14-15).

3. Job got a better righteousness, double riches, more respect, better kids, a happier marriage, and tons of grandchildren. He got an additional 140 years to enjoy all those blessings. See Job 42:10-16. Does that teach that God will reward us likewise for handling our suffering seasons well? Or will we have to wait for eternity? See Hebrews 11:39&40.

4. What do you think about this chapter's statement that some of God's best gifts are unanswered prayers? Compare his complaint of Job 3 with God's goodness in Job 42. Can you think of past prayers never answered to your relief and joy today?

5.   What do you think of the concept of the Distant Happily Ever After? Are you struck by the fact that even 140 years of extra life is still a fleeting moment in eternity's light? See Psalm 90:5-6 & 103:15, Mark 8:36, Luke 16:23, 1 Peter 1:24, James 1:10.

6.   What is your reaction to Lazarus' Distant Happily Ever After? See Luke 16:19-31. Does this balancing of the scales give some answer to the complaint that the righteous suffer while the wicked prosper? Look at the great exchange in 2 Corinthians 4:17 from the perspective of Lazarus, and then the rich man.

7. What was your reaction to Paul finding happiness and power by staying on the ash heap of suffering? See 2 Corinthians 12:6-10. Were you moved by the letter found on the Confederate soldier? Is it just sentimentalism or wisdom for tough times?

8. Where do you find your own Happily Ever After? How does Job's story help? What about Lazarus and the Rich Man? How about St. Paul and the heroes of Hebrews 11?

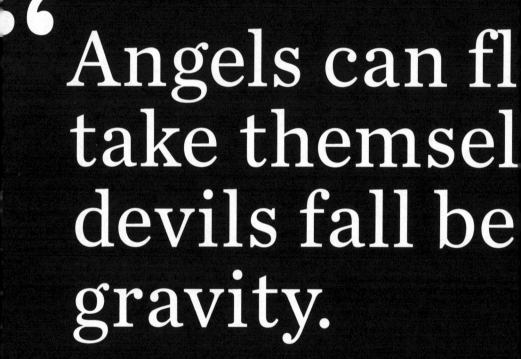

" Angels can fl
take themsel
devils fall be
gravity.

because they
es lightly;
ause of their

"

G.K. Chesterton

Epilogue

ANGELS
ARE WATCHING

ST. PAUL COMES OUT ON stage to remind us of what he says about
The Theater of Angels in his letter to the Ephesians. He now wants
us to see the backdrop to Job's drama; the rest of the story that
never appears in the book of Job.

As the Apostle points to center stage, a single spotlight again
encircles that bag of bones and boils sitting alone on a pile of ashes
in the land of Uz. Then St. Paul magically pulls back a massive
curtain that circles the arena, and we see into the heavenly realms.
A colossal arena surrounds and dwarfs us.

Look! It is filled with myriads of celestial beings. Massive
Seraphim Fire Angels, each with six blazing wings. Faces of dazzling light. Eyes cover their bodies. Feet are ablaze like burning
brass. Cherubim dressed in the purest of white robes. Some
play harps. Others dance rhythmically to some heavenly beat.
Still others sing haunting otherworldly songs. Some emanate
thunder and lightning. There are those with faces like oxen,

others like eagles, a few like lions, and some even like humans. These angelic hosts are a kaleidoscope of shapes, sizes and colors. They are too exotic and fantastic for words to describe. Maybe, if you allow your creativity to run riot, you can see these celestials through your own eyes of imagination.

Across the way, the stands are darker and more sinister. Here sit the fallen angels and their demon offspring. Instead of a kaleidoscope of dazzling colors, one sees shades of grey, faded beauty, and yellowed raggedness where there was once vibrancy. There are no horns, hoofed feet, tails, or pitchforks. Those were Medieval creations designed to keep church folk in line. These celestials look strangely like their heavenly counterparts, except that they are wilted, diminished, and compressed versions. They are after all, *fallen* angels.

Yet there is smoldering energy. Eyes are hot with rage. Lips curl with demonic cruelty, dripping poison that's bubbled up from twisted souls. Bodies are coiled like snakes, compressed with predatory energy, ready to spring with destructive force. Instead of the hauntingly beautiful sounds that swell forth from the angels of heaven, we hear hissing, snarling, snorting, growling, grousing, and complaining. There is laughter, but it comes in response to perverse thought and coarse jesting. Occasionally a song breaks out, but it is like the rowdy drinking song of a drunken mob: crude, shallow, repetitive, and titillating to the carnal senses.

I could ask you to let your imagination run riot again as you peer up into the devil's bleachers, but you would gain no advantage from a long and prolonged look at fallen angels and demons. No one ever wins by focusing on perpetual losers. Besides, St. Paul is calling us to look at the stage, and briefly look at the story from the angels' perspective.

Job's Story through Angels' Eyes

The theater grows eerily quiet. God has set the hook, using righteous Job as the bait. The devil has grabbed it hook-line-and-sinker and countered with the wager: Reduce Job to the ash heap and he will abandon his faith in God. The stakes are stratospherically high. God is staking the integrity of his glory on Job's righteousness. His grace and mercy will be put to the test on Job's ash heap of affliction.

In this standing-room-only crowd, fallen celestials and their half-breed demon offspring grimly hope that they might finally get to watch their dark lord gain a victory. Heaven's angels are puzzled that God would yet again stake his glory and wisdom on a puny clay figure from Uz. Yet they have all flown on fast wings to take their places in the theater. Each wonders, "How will the Most High manage to pull off a victory this time?"

Like all of God's scripts, there are twists and turns of plot that take the audience on a roller-coaster ride. The angels of hell howl in delight when it seems that Job is down for the count. Then he gets up off the canvas again, and the hosts of heaven cheer wildly. It's a back and forth. The thrill of victory is so close, you can almost taste it. Then the agony of defeat is so near that you want to give up.

The Moment of Truth

Now we can hear a pin drop. Job is out on his feet, his faith staggering like a punch drunk fighter on his last legs. He writhes in pain on his ash heap, spewing out crazy talk about God. Fallen angels and demons are hooting and hollering in unbridled ecstasy. Heaven's celestials feel like hiding their faces behind wings, but they can't take their eyes off that black leper on the ash heap. His utter brokenness holds far more fascination for them than his vanilla success in bygone days.

The holy angels have seen heaven's glories, but have never birthed a child or laid one in the grave. They know nothing of the joy of sexual intimacy, or what it's like to be abandoned by a spouse. They have never felt pain, rejection, loneliness, or the degradation of being disfigured.

They know God's holiness, but they have never been touched by his grace. They hear his voice, but will never have his Spirit inside them. They fly on wings of fire, yet don't walk in intimacy with their Creator. They have always worshipped God the Son, but he will never die on a cross for them. Angels long to experience what we humans take for granted. This is why they are so fascinated by Job, and watch us so intently.

Ash heap suffering is beyond anything that they can fathom. The greatest man of the East has been reduced to the hideousness of boils, worms, and pus mingled with blood and soot. His black leprosy makes him look like a gaunt elephant. This is the most wretched man ever been born of a woman. How can the Exalted God of angels and men show his wisdom, power, and goodness in such a miserable clay creature?

God's Triumph

Job bends, but he never breaks. God's grace is tested to the limits, but it never fails. The Man from Uz teeters on the ragged edge, but he never jumps into the abyss of abandoned faith. Satan has unleashed all hell on this ash heap man. But God wraps his arms around Job, and the man from Uz stubbornly holds on to his Redeemer. Neither will let go. This is the only thing that keeps Job from going down for the count. Finally an exhausted

Satan has to throw up his fiery wings in disgust. He whimpers, "No more!" Hell has been utterly defeated. Dark angels and demons quickly exit the theater, gnashing their teeth in rage as they head back to the liquid darkness of unending frustration.

The thunderous applause of those left in The Theater of Angels is deafening. God has shown again that the weakest of clay creatures, filled with his amazing grace, is stronger than the most powerful archangel ever created. Even if that grace is wrapped in disfigurement, doubt, and despair, it is still unbeatable and unstoppable. God has proven that he is all wise, all powerful, and all good in Job's life, just as he has been in the lives of every suffering saint who has ever rubbed the ashes of ruined dreams into the oozing sores of disappointment.

CALVARY'S ASH HEAP

Job's story is made all the more wonderful because it foreshadows another ash heap. St. Paul points to it as Job fades away into the darkness. The spotlight now encircles a twisted and bloody bag of bones impaled on a Roman cross driven deep into a skull-shaped rock heap. This is the ash heap of the ages, and the greatest story of all in The Theater of Angels.

This Roman death machine is the cruelest tool of suffering ever devised by the genius of human depravity. God has written a part for his Son that no human, not even Job, could ever endure. What the devil and evil men do to Jesus is only a small part of his suffering. God the Father piles our sins on his Only Begotten Son until Jesus becomes sin itself. Then he pours out his punishment on his Beloved so that grace can be lavished on us. On this Black Friday he smites his Son with infinitely more affliction than Satan's cruel hate can ever unleash on Job or us.

The God who watches Job bury his children will bury his Only Begotten Son. The Most High who allows Rabbi Kushner to agonize over his son's pain will grieve over the infinitely greater suffering of his Son. Whatever is taken away from Job pales in significance to what our heavenly Father gave away that day. On his ash heap, Job screams at God for ignoring his pain. From his rock pile, Jesus cries out, "My God, My God, why have you forsaken me?" (Matthew 27:46)

God enters into our deepest sufferings at Calvary. He forever redeems our ash heaps by sitting on his own. He knows our pains and empathizes with our suffering. He is able to give us the best comfort that can only be given by a fellow-sufferer. If he would not spare his Only Begotten Son, how can we doubt that he would withhold any grace from his redeemed sons and daughters?

The angels are on the edge of their seats that *Good* Friday. The holy celestials are now weeping as they watch their Beloved Son of God suffer in such agony. We who love our Redeemer cannot watch without joining heaven's angels in their unabashed grief. They must wonder how God the Son can bring salvation to the world by reducing himself to this mangled humanity who looks as disfigured as Job did on his ash heap.

Then Jesus is taken down and buried. Demons howl in delight. Heaven's angels cover their horrified faces. Yet Sunday is coming. On the third day, God the Son rises victoriously from the grave. Job's Redeemer is again in the land of the living.

Look at the celebration that erupts in The Theater of Angels when the gravestone is rolled away and nail-scarred Jesus steps out in Resurrection glory! Angels fly on wings of joy to the empty tomb so they can share the good news with his discouraged followers. The cheering of celestials crescendos in a thunderous roar. Across the way, the section reserved for fallen angels and demons is now silent and dark.

Every time that you rise in victory off your ash heap, it is Resurrection Day all over again in The Theater of Angels. Faith triumphs. God's grace is once again shown to be more than sufficient. You may be barely holding on today, but you will rise again along with Job, Lazarus, St. Paul and all the rest of us who place our hope in the Risen Christ.

What are fallen angels and demons left to do in the light of saints rising repeatedly and triumphantly from their ash heaps of affliction? They slink out of the Theater of Angels, their rage increasing with every defeat. They know that their diabolical efforts are ultimately futile. With each defeat, their doom is made more clear to them. Inflamed by hell's craziness, these devils have nothing left but to prowl the earth, looking for as many clay creatures as possible to rob, destroy, and kill before their Doomsday Clock strikes the hour of their destruction.

Clay Creatures Ablaze with Light

Yet, if you belong to the Resurrected Redeemer, you are a different kind of clay creature. St. Paul was talking about you when he wrote, "But we carry this treasure in clay vessels..." (2 Corinthians 4:7) Like Adam and Eve, you may be made of the earth's clay, but you carry the light of Jesus' presence and power in you. God the Father has given you armor for victorious spiritual warfare. (Ephesians 6:10-17) God the Spirit empowers you to pray great prayers that bring down heaven's power. (Ephesians 6:18) God the Son has promised to stay at your side until the end of this age. (Matthew 28:20) Afflictions will surely come. Some of them will roar straight out of hell itself. Yet they cannot ultimately defeat you. Instead, God will use them to make you stronger for battles ahead while he is sculpting you into the very image of his Jesus Christ.

MY HAPPILY EVER AFTER

I speak with such optimism from experience. When I set the stage in the first chapter, I told you that I would finish my story. The Epilogue is as good a place as any. Of course, my story is still being played out in The Theater of Angels. It has never been a safe merry-go-round ride on a painted pony. I'm glad for that. As long as I can hang on, I want to ride the wild horses to unpredictable places of new adventure.

Please allow me to pick up my story where I left off: A bed wetting 12-year-old boy with the sociability of a four-year-old child, repeatedly abused sexually, diagnosed as unable to receive or give love, shuffled through so many foster homes that I was without a sense of family or name. A sixth grade teacher had written on my report card that I needed to be institutionalized. The summer before that, after I lost brothers that I have never seen since, I shook my fists at the heavens and shouted, "God, I hate you! I hate you!"

Yet the God that I hated loved me before the world was ever created. Even before my birth mom abandoned me, siblings were ripped away, and foster parents broke promises to adopt me, God had already written my name in his family album. Though I will never know the identity of the man who fathered me, from the first moment of conception I belonged to my Father in heaven. Through Christ, I could trace my family tree all the way back to Father Abraham. What a family tree it is: kings, queens, warriors, heroes, prophets, priests, villains, horse thieves, and scoundrels!

Even when I felt forsaken and abandoned, my name was already written in the Lamb's Book of Life because my Father in heaven had already sent his Son to die on a cross for Bobby, the little boy who would never amount to anything. My Happily Ever After was already established even when I was sitting on ash heaps of rejection, shame, and heartache.

Meet the Parents

The very summer that I was shaking my fist at God, Mary Petterson was looking for a little boy and girl. Unable to conceive children of her own because of a childhood disease, she made the rounds of adoption agencies. She wanted babies, but her middle age was against her in those days. So she went to the State Welfare Department, figuring that this agency would be desperate to unload unwanted kids.

Their policies stated that a couple in their mid-forties could only adopt children who were ten years of age, or older. Social workers warned Mary, "These kids have been through the system. By this age, most of them are damaged goods." Mary was not the kind of person to be deterred. Once her mind was made up, no one ever stopped that indomitable woman.

So they brought out an album containing the photographs of some 500 kids who were wards of the court. Mary spent the better part of a day poring over those photos. Then she saw Kim and my pictures. It was love at first sight. "That's the little boy and girl that I want," she said as she continued to gaze at her future son and daughter.

A snowy day just after Christmas will be forever etched in my mind. Mary and Arnold Petterson were coming across the mountains to spend the afternoon with us. Our imperious social worker gave a harsh warning: "Don't mess this up. As old as you are, you may never get another chance at being adopted." What a frightening thing to say to an insecure little boy!

As their car pulled up in the driveway, I grabbed hold of Kimberly's hands. We were dressed in our best rummage sale clothes and scrubbed clean. It was the scariest moment of my life. I was desperate to belong to a *real* family, to have a forever dad and mom, and to own a last name that I could claim for the rest of my life. I surely didn't want to do anything to ruin my last chance at adoption.

Mary jumped out of the car, slipped and slid up the icy sidewalk, until she got to me. She pulled me from the porch and buried my head in her rather ample bosom. I couldn't breathe. It was a most delicious suffocation. Then she let go, looked into my eyes and said, "Bobby, I love you." As far as I can remember, that was the first time that anyone ever said those words with such passion to me. Are there any three words more magical than, "I love you."?

Arnold was more reserved. This quiet Scandinavian was always a man of few words. While Mary poured out her emotions extravagantly and talked incessantly, Arnold shook our hands awkwardly. He wasn't crazy about the idea of adopting two kids. He loved Mary passionately, and didn't want children to interrupt a honeymoon that had lasted for almost two decades. He was a highly successful commercial salmon fisherman, a big outdoorsman who fished the rugged coastlines of Alaska with rough and gruff men of the sea. His massive hands were too big to tie a little girl's shoelaces, and his patience too thin to put up with an insecure boy's mistakes.

We got in the car with our potential parents and went to the bowling alley. I figured that if I bowled a strike they would want to adopt me for sure. As hard as I tried, almost every ball ended up in a gutter. I was sure that I had blown our chances. Then we went to a Chinese restaurant. I don't remember ever dining out before, much less in an Asian eatery. Yet, when I saw those chopsticks, I figured that I could recover from my failed efforts at the bowling alley (Isn't it tragic that so many of us grow up thinking that we have to earn love and acceptance, even from our Father in heaven?).

I tried to pick up some noodles with those sticks, only to have them clumsily crisscross, sending a gooey gob across the table and into Arnold's lap. Everything stopped, including my heart. In that moment of ineptness, I knew that I had lost all hope of adoption. As tears welled up in my eyes, Arnold quietly wiped away the mess on his trousers, and then reached under the table to bring up a model ship that he had painstakingly whittled out of balsa wood over the past weeks. It was a replica of his commercial fishing boat.

At that moment, Mary began to clap her hands. This was their prearranged signal. If Arnold wanted to adopt these kids, he would give the boat to the boy. As he handed me the boat, he said, "Bobby, would you like to be my son?" He then asked my sister if she would like to be his daughter. This was my introduction to grace. My chopstick fiasco couldn't derail Arnold and Mary's love. I think that the mess I made of things endeared me more to them. It's no different with our Father in heaven. He loves us all the more at our messiest moments.

Two weeks later we were on a ferry boat headed out to the Petterson waterfront home on beautiful Orcas Island in the glorious beauty of the Upper Puget Sound. Awaiting me was a

brand-new Roy Roger's cowboy bunk bed in my own room. But
I was deeply troubled as I sat next to Mary in my Davy Crockett
pajamas. I blurted out through tears, "Mom, I wet the bed every
night. I'll ruin these new sheets and mattress. I always do." Mary
put her arms around me and said, "Bobby, your dad and I love
you no matter what. If you wet the bed, we'll change the sheets.
Honey, you're home now. You just go to sleep and dream sweet
dreams." That night, I fell asleep in a peace I'd never known. As
dawn broke, I awoke in a dry and warm bed. I never again wet
the bed. Grace is amazing!

We went to our little schoolhouse the next day. My parents
were leading citizens of the island, so our adoption was hot
news. Yet the school playground can be the cruelest place on
earth. Jealous classmates teased us: "You're not real kids like us.
You're adopted." I think that this was my first encounter with
existentialism. I had always thought I was real. However, the
great snare of my childhood (and plague of so many folk) was
allowing other people to define me. That night, I told my new
mom what our classmates had said about Kim and me. Mary
cuddled me close and said with a chuckle, "Bobby, those kids'
parents had to take what they got at the hospital. We went out
and looked for you. We chose you out all the children in the world.
You and your sister are the most special of all because you are
chosen children."

Grace turns to Works

I would like to say that those idyllic days were our Happily Ever
After, but that only happens in fairy tales. The case workers were
right: Both Kim and I were damaged goods. At our respective ages
of ten and twelve we were already hard wired with insecurities,

deceptive thinking, and dysfunctional ways of dealing with danger and disappointment. It took little for me to go into a fetal position. Like most kids coming out of the foster care system, I lived in fear that I would mess up in some way that would make my new parents give me back to the foster care system. So I became the chronic people pleaser. Like most kids who have learned to survive in dangerous relationships, I could read quickly what others needed me to be in order to keep them happy and me safe. By 13 years of age, I had the equivalent of a Masters Degree in manipulation and a PH.D in deception, along with a collection of masks that could be changed at a moment's notice.

Mostly, I retreated into books that took me to faraway places, and spent hours trekking the beaches and forests where my vivid imagination could create worlds where I was a mighty warrior, brave soldier, Prince Charming, or the adored king who made all his subjects rich and happy .

I wish I could say that Arnold and Mary were model parents. They loved us with a flawed love. I know now that they did the best they could. Mary was determined to reshape us into her image of what model kids should be. For the most part, Arnold worked on his fishing nets and left the child-rearing to Mary. She could be brutal in her expectations and harsh in her corporal punishment. Her exuberance for life was too often unbridled and even out-of-control passion. To give her credit, she believed that she could achieve the impossible of undoing in a few years the damage that had been done to her adopted kids over several years in abuse.

Kim had a hard time with school; Mary was determined that she would get good grades. She never knew that Kim was dyslexic. Kim was chubby; Mary was determined that she would be a cute little cheerleader. Life was often a continuing contest of wills between Kimberly and Mary. As hard as Kim tried, she could never do enough. Those unrequited efforts finally broke Kim's spirit. After years of a deteriorating relationship, mom parted ways with Kimberly. She never spoke to her adopted daughter again. Long after Mary went to be with Jesus, Kim's heart still aches with the pain of that rejection.

My sister and I spent years apart, as she and I went separate ways to find our healing. We have been reunited in recent years. Our newfound relationship is precious to me. She still carries scars and enduring pain as she tries to figure out what went wrong. Yet her resilient spirit brings great joy to my life. That is why I have dedicated this book to this uncommon woman who is redeeming her ash heap afflictions.

I responded differently than Kimberly. Whereas she courageously fought back, my defense mechanism was to make everyone happy. As a newly adopted kid, I was determined to be just like my big fisherman dad. I took "Arnold" as my middle name. I dressed just like my dad, took on his mannerisms, and aped his every move. As I walked down the fishing docks beside my dad, mimicking him in every way possible, fisherman working on their nets would call out my pop's nickname: "Here comes Pete and his son Re-Pete."

If my parents, teachers, or classmates asked me to jump, my response was always, "How high?" And then I would leap higher than expected. I was constantly figuring out how to earn acceptance and applause. My dysfunction was much more socially acceptable than my sister's refusal to play the game. It resulted in top grades, athletic awards, starring roles in school plays, kudos at church, and Arnold and Mary's praise.

The Boy is the Father of the Man

This drive for perfection followed me through the years. It made me a control freak, causing me to drive myself and fix others. As a husband, I micro-managed my wife. As a father, I withheld emotion from my daughter when she didn't react the way I wanted. As a pastor, I thought that it was my job to make sure that everyone stayed in the church, and did so happily. Yet no preacher can make all the people happy all the time. When people left the church, I spent days in an emotional fetal position. Then I would get up, grit my teeth, and charge forward with renewed determination to prove myself to God, myself, and everyone else.

I earned a doctorate, but didn't feel any smarter. I became a gifted preacher and sought after speaker, both at home and abroad. My story became the catalyst for thousands to come to Christ. However, there was no joy in my heart. Even as my churches grew, I lived in constant fear that they might collapse at any moment. I felt God's pleasure in me when I preached and taught, and listeners were captivated by my passion and insights. I earned the nickname "Bouncy Bob." Yet, beneath the bubbly exterior lurked the little boy with fears and sadness that had never been resolved. If people could have seen me when I was not on stage, they might have called me "Brooding Bob."

I tried to stuff my hurts by misapplying St. Paul's words, "This one thing I do, forgetting what lies behind and straining toward what lies ahead, I press on..." (Philippians 3:12&14) For years I refused to find Kimberly, or even crack open the door to the past, lest sleeping wolves might rise to howl again.

The Downward Road to Deliverance

Then I hit rock bottom. One can only juggle the balls for so many years before they come crashing down. A church split sent me into a downward spiral ending in suicidal depression. Anxiety kept me awake for days and nights on end. I begged God for sleep that never came. In exhausted desperation, I turned to prescription drugs. They brought sleep, but no rest. All the time, I was playing the smiley-faced preacher in the pulpit. Yet people of discernment knew better.

On the ragged edge of giving up, I was introduced to a quadriplegic Christian psychologist. Thank God, he was not one of Job's comforters. His years on an ash heap of paralysis made him an unusually empathetic counselor. Over months of intensive therapy I began to see deceptions and lies that had governed my thinking since childhood. Slowly, with a heaping helping of God's grace and my wife's encouragement, I began to climb out of the pit.

Years later, I can say that I am in a far better place, as is my marriage, family, and ministry. When I was reunited with Kim, she shared an amazing thing that she discovered about our past. Our grandmother was a wild child in a village in Maine. As a teen she ran off with a traveling gypsy. A few months later she came home pregnant. The gypsy had abandoned her.

The wild child's sweetheart married her to cover her shame. Yet he never accepted the baby girl born from that union with the gypsy. Her very existence was a constant reminder of her mother's unfaithfulness. Unloved by her stepfather, she went looking for love in all the wrong places. She too became pregnant as an unwed teen. I was that child born of a neediness that she never satisfied in a lifetime of searching for love.

A couple of years after discovering this family secret, I was ministering to a conference of Dalit pastors in India. The Dalit peoples number 350 million. They are the outcasts of the Hindu caste system. For centuries they have been the victims of the most oppressive apartheid in the world. But today Holy Spirit winds are blowing across India. More outcasts and low cast people have come to Christ in the past fifteen years in India than the whole number of converts in the first six centuries of Christianity. This may well be the greatest evangelistic movement in history. Our Covenant Church of Naples has been the partner church to the Good Shepherd Church Movement that is at the heart of this great gospel explosion in India. I have had the privilege of being designated the pastor-at-large to thousands of pastors and church planters of the Good Shepherd Churches.

After teaching at a large training conference, a group of pastors said to me, "You are different than most Westerners. You understand our pain. You speak to us as a brother who has experienced our suffering." I told them my story, including the part about my grandmother who ran off with the gypsy.

Dr. Joseph D'Souza, Bishop of the Good Shepherd Churches, grabbed hold of my hands afterwards, and excitedly said, "Bob, do you know what you've just said?" Then he began to tell me that the gypsies are originally from India. Millions still live on the subcontinent. They were scattered across Central Asia by the Mogul invaders from Persia in the 13th Century. Later Genghis Khan's hoard drove them westward into Europe. There they were known as the Romani. They became mysterious figures in literature, and often despised as thieves and vagabonds. Adolf Hitler singled them out as one of the groups for liquidation. More gypsies percentage wise were killed in the holocaust than Jews. Many have immigrated to America where more than a million live today. The father of my mother was one of them.

When the shock wore off, Dr. D'Souza looked at me and

quipped, "The gypsies of India are also outcasts. That makes you a Dalit too." I responded, "That's okay. I've felt like an outcast and vagabond most of my life." Later, when the assembled pastors were told that I was of gypsy parentage and an outcast, they began to cheer wildly. I giddily announced to them, "I've been looking for my lost brothers all my life. Now I've found them here in India." As one man, hundreds rushed forward to embrace me. I felt like I had come home at last.

A few days later I was in a jetliner taking off from the Hyderabad, India airport. I began to belly laugh with a joy I had never felt before. My missionary partner, Dave Berg, asked why this sudden outburst of joy. I replied, "Who would have known that, when a wild child in Maine ran off with a traveling gypsy, eighty years later she would have set in motion a series of events that would put her grandson in the middle of the greatest evangelistic and liberation movement in history?"

Those events have put folks on thousands of ash heaps of affliction. They have been painful beyond belief. Yet, for the first time in my life, they made sense. A wise God has woven together a history, using the sins and stupidities of flawed and fallen people, to bring about good for so many millions more. It couldn't have happened without his power. We can count it all joy when we see the goodness of his severe mercy.

I would try your patience, dear friend, if I were to recount the many pains and sorrows that have been inflicted on me by others, including the most pious of Christians. I would be ashamed to confess how much pain and disappointment that little Bobby has inflicted on others while walking this road to glory. The journey still has its moments. The wolves still rise up and howl occasionally, but they sleep so much longer now.

I know that there are ash heap seasons ahead. Eliphaz was right when he said that we are born for trouble. However, I prefer to hold close to my heart the words of St. Paul: 'We are more than conquerors through him who loved us." (Romans 8:37) I can triumphantly affirm with Job, "Even though the Lord slay me, yet will I hope in him." (Job 13:15)

KEEP ON SHINING, THE ANGELS ARE WATCHING

The Son of Light Bringer thought himself to be demoted and demeaned to have to guard the clay creatures in Eden. He couldn't see that the things God calls us to do are so much better than the vain things we imagine for ourselves. Ash heaps of suffering fall into that category. We can sum up everything that God calls us to experience in the title of a golden oldie television sitcom: Father Knows Best.

Lucifer didn't know true worth when he saw it. What he dismissed as puny clay figures crawling along the dust of the earth were the treasures of God. St. Paul calls us jars of clay in 2 Corinthians 4:7. Yet God chose to fill us with a light that far surpasses the radiant glory of angels. He fills us with the Holy Spirit who brings the presence and power of "...the true Light who gives light to everyone..." (John 1:9)

Lucifer could never understand how clay creatures could hold a light far more dazzling and explosive than his own. The angels couldn't understand how a black leper, scraping himself with chards of broken clay pottery, could show that light, or how the crucified Messiah could burst forth from a tomb with Resurrection glory that would bring light to the people who walk in darkness.

They will never quite get us either. That's why they keep watching when we are hard-pressed on every side, but not crushed;

persecuted, but never alone; beaten on, but never destroyed. (2 Corinthians 4:8&9) The clay is cracked, pockmarked, chipped, and showing signs of strain and age. Sometimes it is covered with boils and stained with soot. Some will look at a fragile little clay jar called Bobby Bedwetter, and say, "That little boy will never amount to anything." Yet a flickering light within will someday light up the darkness.

Dear friend, it's in the fires that clay pots are hardened and made ready to carry water, food, or even fire. Without the fire, the clay pot will never be useful or stand the pressures of life. Yet the fire always leaves behind ashes that we must sit on.

May the Light shine brightly in you, redeemed clay creature. May all your moments on the center stage in the Theater of Angels be those that make you go from glory to glory until that day when all of heaven will stand on tiptoe to look at you with awe, the finished masterpiece of his workmanship. I can hardly wait to stand there with you as all heaven applauds God's glory that is in each of us.

It is customary for books, plays, and movies to wrap up with those familiar lines: THE END. But it's never the end for any of us. So we will conclude with those words of eternal hope:

"The Beginning"

STORIES
SET IN STONE

A STUDY GUIDE

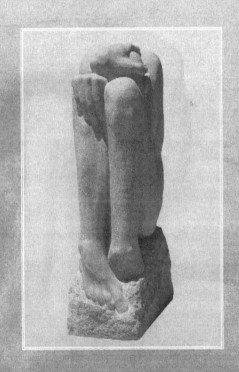

We take a last look a Claudia's sculpture. Job is frozen in stone, beckoning us to come back again and again to his story. Though his suffering was epic, he only had one ash heap experience. We are more blessed than Job. We will have several ash heap seasons, giving us far more opportunities to show the death, burial, and resurrection of Jesus Christ.

If every person's story is everyone else's story, then Job's is yours. More importantly, Christ's story is yours too. We are part of a troupe of players; the fraternity of the suffering who show something of God's great wisdom, power, and goodness to watching angels and people. This gives our life great significance. Let's again meditate on what that means, and share those thoughts with one another.

1. Take a short time to let your imagination run riot. What do you think the angels in the surrounding arena would look like if you could pull back the curtain that hides the invisible realms? See Genesis 3:24, Isaiah 6:2, Ezekiel 28:13, Daniel 7:2&10:5-6, Genesis 19:1-18, Matthew 28:4, Hebrews 13:2, Revelation 4:7-8 & 10:1-3. What about the fallen angels and demons?

2. Angels are fascinated by us and our struggles. What do they possess that we don't? See Psalm 8:5 and Hebrews 2:7. What do we possess that they never will? What do we experience that they never will?

3. Does Job triumph because he holds on to God or God holds on to him? Is it either **God**? See John 10:27-30. Or **you**? See James 4:8. Or is it **both**? See Philippians 2:13&14. To put it another way, should we call this the perseverance of the saints or God's perseverance with the saints?

4. What do you make of the statement that the weakest of God's
    creatures filled with grace is stronger than the mightiest of his
    archangels? Do you believe that of yourself? See I Corinthians
    1:26-30, I John 4:4, James 4:7, 2 Corinthians 2:11 & 10:4, Ephesians
    6:10-18, Revelation 12:11.

    _____

    _____

    _____

    _____

    _____

    _____

    _____

    _____

5. How does Job's ash heap story foreshadow the death, burial,
    and resurrection of Christ? How can your suffering show the
    watching world (and angels) more about Jesus than your words? See
    2 Corinthians 3:3 & 4:10, Philippians 1:21.

    _____

    _____

    _____

    _____

    _____

    _____

    _____

    _____

6. Why is it Resurrection Day all over again for the angels every time we triumph over our suffering? See Ephesians 3:10&11. On the other hand, how do our triumphs send a message to devils that their doom is sure?

_____

_____

_____

_____

_____

_____

7. What did you think of Bob Petterson's story? What did you learn from it? Can you think of past hurts that have made a difference in your present life and in ministering to others?

_____

_____

_____

_____

_____

_____

8. What does it mean to be a clay creature with a blazing light inside? 2 Corinthians 4:7. When Gideon's 300 man army threw down their clay pots filled with light, breaking them into pieces, they routed a massive army. See Judges 7:16-17. Do you see that as a picture of what Christ can do with you and the church today?

_____

_____

9. What do you make of the last line of The Theater of Angels:

"The Beginning"?

DESERT

TRANSFORMED BY TRIBULATIONS

CROSSINGS

ROBERT PETTERSON